BOOKS BY CAROLE SPEARIN MCCAULEY

NONFICTION
Pregnancy after 35
Surviving Breast Cancer
AIDS: Prevention and Healing with Nutrition
Computers and Creativity

FICTION
Happenthing in Travel On
The Honesty Tree
Six Portraits

When Your Child Is Afraid

DR. ROBERT SCHACHTER
AND
CAROLE SPEARIN McCAULEY

SIMON AND SCHUSTER
New York · London · Toronto · Sydney · Tokyo

Copyright © 1988 by Dr. Robert Schachter and
Carole Spearin McCauley
All rights reserved
including the right of reproduction
in whole or in part in any form.
Published by Simon and Schuster
A Division of Simon & Schuster Inc.
Simon & Schuster Building
Rockefeller Center
1230 Avenue of the Americas
New York, NY 10020

SIMON AND SCHUSTER and colophon are registered trademarks
of Simon & Schuster Inc.

Designed by: Helen L. Granger/Levavi & Levavi
Manufactured in the United States of America

3   5   7   9   10   8   6   4   2

Library of Congress Cataloging in Publication Data
Schachter, Robert.
When your child is afraid / Robert Schachter and
Carole Spearin McCauley.

p.   cm.
Bibliography: p.
Includes index.
1. Phobias in children.   I. McCauley, Carole Spearin.   II. Title.
RJ506.P38S33   1988
649'.1'019—dc 19   87-35615
CIP
ISBN 0-671-62683-3

Acknowledgments

I want to thank the people who have helped to make this book possible. In this case there are two groups, my family and those professionals who have contributed to my understanding of the science and art of helping people. My wife, Wendi, as always has been great. It is her encouragement that started me on this endeavor and her inspiration that kept me at it. My parents and in-laws, Michael and Sydel Lazar, have been extremely supportive and also have all my appreciation.

In terms of professionals, there are a few people I have been fortunate to meet who have truly made a difference in helping me understand the work I do. It started at Tufts University with the dean of the graduate school, Kathryn McCarthy, who first gave me an opportunity to prove myself in this field. Dr. Jean Wellington, who first introduced me to group therapy, gave me the basics of my knowledge. Dr. Eileen Nickerson helped me get through my doctoral program in one and a half years and, with her enthusiasm and dedication to the field, gave me the support to get me started. And finally, I wish to thank a wonderful pediatrician, Dr. Virginia Pomeranz, who is no longer with us. She helped me start my practice after I moved to New York and showed me an understanding of medicine and a dedication to her patients that I've always appreciated. She was the one who was able to sense what was wrong with a child in addition to just following pat lines. She helped parents cut through the mumbo jumbo of illness and spoke to them in plain English.

This book was a pleasure to write. It wasn't the standard

horror of endless nights and painful, wordless days, and I hope it can help a few parents who are struggling with the helplessness of watching the young people they love be afraid.

—Dr. Robert Schachter

To Ilana, my beautiful daughter, who is a never ending inspiration to her old dad.

—DR. ROBERT SCHACHTER

Dedicated to parents and others who need sensible answers to hard questions at 3 A.M. when all our monsters loom.

—CAROLE SPEARIN McCAULEY

A Note to Parents

The intent of this book is to aid you in sorting out some of the fears of your child. In order to have a chronological order we listed these as they exist with most children.

All people are individuals, however. Some of the fears may overlap so that although we are listing a particular fear for a six-year-old, you may observe it in your four-year-old. Our reference is a general one.

I hope you find this a helpful approach to understanding that which is quite often inscrutable.

Contents

PART II: PHOBIAS

Many lamentable effects this fear causeth in
humans, as to be red, pale, tremble, sweat; it makes
sudden cold and heat to come all over the body,
palpitation of the heart, syncope. . . . They that live
in fear are never free, resolute, secure, merry, but in
constant pain . . . no greater misery, no rack, no
torture, like unto it.
>   —THOMAS BURTON,
>   *The Anatomy of Melancholy,*
>   1621

Fear is the foundation of safety.
>   —TERTULLIAN, c.220 A.D.

CHAPTER 1

. . .

Introduction:
Fears Are
Windows . . .

The Browns were a happy young couple raising their first child. Jessica—a beautiful, blond, blue-eyed girl, twenty-one months old—charmed everyone she met. She could count; she knew her colors; and her smile seemed to light the entire world in a minute.

After Jessica reached twenty months, however, she began waking in the middle of the night. Standing up, she would start to cry for her mother and demand to leave her crib. When her parents entered her room to reassure her that they were nearby, she would not be quieted. After they left her room, she became so agitated she would jump or fall from the crib.

Following several of these heart-shuddering thumps, her parents put her into a junior bed. Nevertheless, she continued to wake, scream, and run into her parents' room four or five times a night.

Both John and Ann Brown worked a full day that began at eight each morning. All they could do was to hope that Jessica would soon overcome her wakefulness. When she didn't, her father finally called the pediatrician, who said to be firm with Jessica and keep her in her own room. Each night then became a weary battle, both parents dreading 2 A.M., when Jessica began her nightly travail. Each morning as they exhaustedly roused themselves from bed, they found a happy, delighted child who acted as if she'd not missed one moment's sleep.

Although the Browns began to fight about how to stop this nightly torture, they could devise no way to stop their lovely daughter's predawn screams.

What this family experienced was a form of *separation anxiety,* which often occurs in children twenty-one months old. What Jessica suffered was a reaction to waking alone, of sensing herself in the dark, cut off from her parents. As we shall see later, such a fear is typical of this age; Jessica's fear was separation anxiety.

· · ·

This is a book about children's fears—both normal and abnormal. It is designed first of all to help you as a parent or teacher understand these various fears in your child or in children with whom you work.

Second, it will help you distinguish which of these fears are normal and will be outgrown from those that are more serious and require professional assistance.

Third, you will receive concrete help—what to say and do —to alleviate each major group of fears. Indeed, knowing about your child's fears and learning what you can do to help reassure a frightened youngster is one of the most useful skills a parent can have. For most parents, identifying the behavior as a sign of normal fear is reassuring, especially if the child cannot or will not admit to being afraid.

We, the authors of this book, are a knowledgeable team of psychologist Dr. Robert Schachter and medical and science writer, editor, and novelist Carole Spearin McCauley. Throughout Dr. Schachter's years of practice with children and adolescents, he and other therapists at Robert Schachter Associates, New York City, have seen thousands of children who are afraid. Most of these fears, of course, are normal and part of normal development. An eight-year-old confides that he is terrified of the ghost in his closet. A fourteen-year-old boy discusses his fear of heights. A sixteen-year-old confides his dread of walking down a dark street.

Although these are "normal" children, the quality and tone of their fears are urgent and feel enormous at the time. We know that such fears pass as children mature, but it is fascinating how many fears persist throughout childhood. Depending on how a parent handles these, the youngster can emerge feeling secure and safe or can stay imprisoned for years in a "normal" world of fears.

Child psychiatrist Benjamin Wolman estimates that 90 percent of normal children, like Jessica, develop fears "appropriate to their age." Material from other studies shows that fully one half of all children fear dogs, dark, thunder, and ghosts, and of this group 10 percent have two or more serious fears (phobias).

Does all this fear serve any purpose, other than ensuring that horror movies by certain producers will always find packed audiences? What function do emotions, including fear, actually serve in the human psyche? When we researched the history of "the twilight zone," what did we find? For the developing child, normal fears are adaptive.

Most people usually consider fear to be bad, since it certainly doesn't *feel* good. Do you recall the sinking sensation in the pit of your stomach, your breath growing shorter, while your spine tingled as the muddy Horror from the Swamp lurched toward you on the movie screen? Or even the last time you entered a totally dark house?

Yet when we pass from the "what" to the "why" of fear, we discover that fear is a practical, useful emotion. Throughout the evolution of humankind, organs and characteristics that aid individual survival are retained, whereas those such as the appendix, a substantial tail, and masses of body hair have atrophied or disappeared. Our emotions have remained with us, and they do serve worthy purposes.

Fear has always warned both animals and humans of danger. From the time of our prehistoric mammalian heritage, fear has functioned as an adaptive signal system to alert us to hazards, prompting us to either fight or flee a dangerous situation. Without necessarily encouraging cowardice, fear helped humans survive.

In 1897, G. Stanley Hall, having researched 1,701 college students, published "A Study of Fears" in the *American Journal of Psychology*. When he discovered that a very few categories —animals, water, death, disease—could encompass the majority of fears and that fear of snakes headed both the most frequent list and the animal list, he noted that contemporary fears still reflect past conditions better than current ones. Persistence of some fears indicates "a peculiar prepotent quality . . . that suggests some ancient origin."

In the early part of this century, various modern theories, particularly those formulated by psychologists J. Lange and W. B. Cannon, elaborated on the physiological survival value of fear. In 1929 in *Bodily Changes in Pain, Hunger, Fear, and Rage,* Cannon described the now well-known effect of released adrenaline to mobilize the sympathetic nervous system, heart, liver, and muscles to achieve rapid action.

Other researchers, like K. M. B. Bridges, have seen various emotions, including fear, as products of a child's maturation and learning process. After observing groups of children longitudinally or chronologically, they concluded that emotional reaction and expression depend on maturation of brain, facial and body muscles, and vocal apparatus. First comes the startle response (closed eyes, rigid neck, thrust chin) after a loud noise or sudden movement. Indeed, Katherine Bridges ("Emotional Development in Early Infancy," *Child Development*) called this response "the most primitive of all emotional patterns, more consistent from one person to another than any other emotional pattern." At three to six months the basic emotions of excitement, delight, and distress modulate to include elation, fear, disgust, and anger.

For these two reasons, then—maturation and survival—fear can be considered a healthy, normal emotion, as when a child encounters a new or unfamiliar situation—the first day of school, an evening with a different baby-sitter. Such fears are common, usually pass quickly, and can even be expected as children mature in age and experience the world. A toddler who screams that a vacuum cleaner or lawn mower will chase him because "it doesn't like me" or it's "noisy," "angry," or "mean" needs to understand the difference between animate and inanimate objects. And his parents need to know that such fears are usual and do not reflect upon the quality of their parenting—or their vacuuming. Similarly, a five-year-old fears ghosts and other imaginary creatures, while an eleven-year-old much more realistically fears for the safety of himself and his loved ones. (Incidentally, "Sesame Street"'s lovable Cookie Monster, at whom children can *laugh,* has much decreased fears in the "monster" category, according to a 1973 New York University study by C. C. Lynch.)

Some experts would even say that no adult—including psychological researchers—can truly empathize with a child's fear or rage unless he returns to the power, impotence, and horror of dream or nightmare states. At the very least, parents should remember that children are not merely miniature adults, possessing the same fears in smaller packages; it is too easy to forget how the world looks from the viewpoint of a fragile child, the fairy-tale Jack in a world of giants and towering beanstalks. Further confusion can arise because the content of a youngster's fears can change month to month, year to year, as the child's mind and abilities mature toward independence.

To guide you, here are some working definitions:

Fear is an unpleasant emotion that occurs in response to a consciously recognized source of danger—real or imaginary.

Its physiological symptoms are rapid pulse rate and respiration, raised blood pressure, increased muscular tension. It is no wonder that treating mental fears aids physical health, as demonstrated in research with teenage diabetics and other teenagers whose previously elevated blood pressure remained lowered after sessions dealing with their fears.

Anxiety is a disturbing feeling of impending doom when there is no specifically feared object or circumstance. Shortness of breath, dizziness, a sinking in the stomach, and rapid heartbeat are all symptoms.

A *phobia* is a fear that does not pass after a short adjustment period and that disturbs the child's functioning. In some children it becomes a constant, compulsive preoccupation with avoiding the feared object or event, as shown by a five-year-old boy who, scared by seeing a comic-book character with shrunken hands, avoided candy stores because they sell comics.

The very origins of these three English words show how ancient they are and how well our ancestors—from three different cultures—differentiated them:

> Fear, from Old English *faer*, peril.
> Anxiety, from Latin *anxius*, troubled, and *angere*,
> to choke.
> Phobia, from ancient Greek *phobos*, dread.

· · ·

Obviously you know your own youngsters better than any professional who sees them infrequently, but you may need help both with the detective work of discerning what's wrong and with concrete dialogues on everything from ghosts and German shepherds to nuclear war.

This book will help you understand the often terrifying world of the normal, healthy child. Our chapters also contain methods developed and tested at the Children's Phobia Center in New York City for handling your children's fears and upsets *before* they become family-disruptive phobias or permanent neuroses. Should you, too, still fear elevators, large dogs, or Monday mornings, there's some sensible self-help for you here as well. As any instructor knows, you can't teach anything without making it part of yourself first.

To parents unused to admitting or evaluating their own emotions, these methods may seem threatening at first. However, in Chapter 11 (Further Hints: What to Do If—) we will help parents sort out their own possible terrors and clarify their own motivations about helping children with fears. For now, we assure you *the payoff is a child who can finally cope with fear.* And your child's self-esteem will increase directly in proportion to success with the methods.

Besides our original contribution to children's fear literature in the form of this book, we wish to acknowledge the decades of study on all aspects of childhood development, including fears, achieved by Dr. Arnold Gesell and his staff at the Gesell Institute, New Haven, Connecticut. Although the content of fears is partly universal and historic (snakes, heights, fire, and so forth), it is also culturally determined. We have therefore ranged beyond the universal to include those fears that are the norm for many children in our noisy, complicated, technological and Western society that favors machinery, lengthy schooling, busy families, time and social pressures upon everyone.

A norm, of course, is an average. If your child attends school happily, for instance, with little sign of separation anxiety at three, six, or ten but instead exhibits it at fourteen when starting private school away from home, he is probably responding to the particulars of your situation. After all, not everybody *must* dread dinosaurs or tigers at exactly age five!

· · ·

According to a fear survey schedule done in the mid-sixties by J. Wolpe and P. J. Lang, the following are the fifteen most common human fears (not arranged according to frequency). Do any of them resonate in you? Which do you see in your child?

Public speaking	Dentists, injections
Making mistakes	Hospitals, open wounds, blood
Failure	Taking tests
Disapproval	Police
Rejection	Dogs
Angry people	Spiders
Being alone	Deformed people
Darkness	

According to one study done by the National Institutes of Health in 1983, alcohol abuse and simple phobias—not depression—have become the "most common lifetime mental health disorders in the general population." According to data from Dr. Barry Wolfe, of the National Institute of Mental Health, phobias affect as many as 25 million people in the United States, of whom 12 million are agoraphobic (fear open spaces, a condition related to separation anxiety).

Of course, ordinary fears afflict many others, not only the definitively phobic. The point, however, is that many of these fears originate normally in childhood and then go unrecognized and untreated and develop into more serious phobias later.

We should hasten to add that much of our experience and research for this book was not limited to the terrors of the twilight zone. Some fears and human reactions to them are actually humorous, even if the wisdom gained stems from hysteria recollected in tranquillity. Some people, paradoxically, actually overdo what they fear most. Here is the incomparable Peter Ustinov at twelve, "conquering" his twin fears of heights and water in his autobiography, *Dear Me:*

Already at Mr. Gibbs' school I had become sickened by my own cowardice, my squeamishness in the face of pain, my panic when confronted by strange dogs or flying cricket balls, and I had deliberately—to my watching mother's horror—entered the school diving competition without knowing the first thing about it. I had climbed up to the highest diving board, and with all the school and all the parents watching, there was no way back. From up there I saw the green water below, which looked much like a stamp on an envelope, and I wondered what guarantee there was that I would not miss the water altogether and end up a red smudge on the gleaming tiles. Taking myself by surprise—it was the only way to do it —I made a graceful gesture in the air, rather like the Rolls-Royce mascot, and fell, a tangled ball of flesh, until I heard a tremendous explosion and fingers of chlorine bored their way brutally into my nostrils. My stomach felt as though it had been unzipped. "You must remember to keep your feet together," called out the expert, but I could hardly hear him over the wailing sirens in my ears.

In this case, such sink-and-swim technique is an example of what psychologists call *counterphobic behavior*. Had Mr. Ustinov been gradually desensitized to some of his normal fears of dogs and balls, however, he would have missed one of his earliest grand performances, and the world would have missed both a good story and a ray of light into a human soul.

· · ·

In summary, the pediatrician T. Berry Brazelton has written in his book *To Listen to a Child*, "Fears can be seen as a window into the inevitable periods of adjustment which all children must go through."

May this book open the window to understanding a fundamental aspect of your children's growth.

How to Use
This Book

In this and the following chapters, for each age (year) we list the typical or normal fears that characterize it. You will find this material in the accompanying boxes, which also serve as summaries for quick reference. From each list we then expand on salient items from the chief fear groups (visual, spatial, social, natural, and so forth) as they affect a particular year or age group. Do note that some items, such as fears of animals or monsters, extend over more than one age category. Within each chapter we have arranged the fear sections both by age and by fear group. So the infant's anxieties about strangers and separation logically cluster together, as do the older child's fears of injury from natural events (including animals) or the teenager's social woes regarding popularity and gossip.

As the child grows, his "fear repertoire" also expands. Although the *content* of the fear (animals, the dark, and so forth) may remain constant, the child's *reaction* or response will vary by age and maturity. Upon seeing a German shepherd, a frightened two-year-old will cry and hide in mother's skirt. A ten-year-old may shout, flee, or pretend to fling a rock at the dog. Because the repertoire of responses is larger, the recommendations (What to Do sections) change year by year.

For quick summary by age: Consult boxes and the Fear Survey Chart at the end of this book.

For detailed information, including anecdotes: See individual fear sections.

PART I

·

Normal
Fears

·

CHAPTER 2

· · ·

In the Beginning: Fears of Babies and Toddlers (Birth to Three Years Old)

TYPICAL FEARS DURING THE FIRST YEAR

Fears in the first twelve months of life are solidly based on both vulnerability and biology, for infancy is the time when a baby needs to learn basic trust in the environment and its caretakers. Fears nevertheless surface around separation, strangers, sudden noises, loss of support (falling), sleep, animals, and medical visits.

See sections below for detailed treatment and What to Do about each of these fears.

"MOMMY, DON'T GO!": SEPARATION ANXIETY
(BIRTH TO THREE YEARS OLD)

Does the following ever happen when you leave for, or return from, a day's work—or from any absence at all, however brief?

Mary and Joe were a happy new family with their daughter, Joanne, who, following a perfect pregnancy and birth, seemed the ideal child. To allow time for a baby, Mary had taken a one-year leave of absence from her job as a computer programmer. Because she enjoyed full-time mothering, she and Joanne had become good friends and companions for play, walks, and socializing with other mothers and babies. Moreover, Mary and Joe, once a couple, were now joyfully a family of three.

Before the end of her year's absence, Mary and Joe interviewed ten baby-sitters for little Joanne, finally choosing a kind, stable woman who, as a professional nanny in England, had cared for children all her work life. Both wife and husband considered her the ideal person. Mary thus carefully planned her reentry into the kind of work for which she had spent years educating herself. As much as she loved Joanne, she anticipated resuming the rest of her adult life.

On Mary's first day away, Joanne seemed to adjust superbly to the new caretaker, who reported that the baby was cooing and playing when Mary phoned.

After Mary rushed home from work that day, eager to hug her little girl, Joanne merely continued playing with her blocks and Raggedy Ann doll. She scarcely glanced at Mary; indeed, for the first hour it seemed as if Mary weren't there. The nanny had left for the day, and Joe hadn't arrived.

Suddenly Joanne began screeching and sobbing in a way Mary had never seen. Clinging to her mother like a little koala bear, she finally fell asleep whimpering in her mother's arms. Devastated, Mary knew that despite her careful plans, her leaving was causing deep disturbance. Now wavering between extending her leave of absence and dismissing the nanny she'd tried so hard to find, she phoned the pediatrician. When he advised that she return to work the next day no matter how badly she felt, she realized she felt even worse.

When she could not sleep that night, Joe knew neither how to calm her nor how to solve Joanne's situation.

As morning came, a sleepless Mary braved herself and left the house. When she phoned from the office, she was astounded to hear that Joanne once again was cooing quietly while she and the baby-sitter played.

Following Mary's return from work that night, however, the same desperate scene replayed itself. Joanne continued to give her mother a hard time for several days.

Definition

Although this distress can assume various forms, ranging from that of Jessica (in Chapter 1), who awakens fearfully in the dark, to the anger and depression experienced by a child who feels abandoned during prolonged separation, its usual form varies from a mild to a severe reaction in a child either after the parent(s) have left the child in someone else's care or upon their return. Without successful intervention, painful scenes will recur, and such fear can also spread to the child's nap or bedtime.

In this youngest age group separation anxiety may occur typically at about eight, thirteen, twenty, and twenty-four months. After it peaks, around the middle of the second year, it usually begins to decline and may end by the child's third birthday. If it reappears at later ages, particularly six to ten years, it is typically associated with fears of going to school.

At each age the child's developmental stage determines the nature of the separation fear. Before eight months, for example, the baby believes that if mother disappears, she will never return. As the baby matures and the image of mother becomes more permanent, this fear abates. When walking begins, how-ever, the child realizes that she can now wander away from mother, thus creating a different kind of separation fear based on personal responsibility.

Although the child primarily fears leaving the caretaking parent, she may alternate between keeping angry distance and sudden clinginess beyond imagining. The most difficult aspect for the parents is experiencing the child's vulnerability, since they suffer from their own guilt and sense of loss at leave-taking.

Some form of separation anxiety occurs in all children, but individual youngsters, particularly those children who have not previously experienced absence, can have a worse time of it. In our example, part of Joanne's distress stemmed from her utter shock that her mother could leave her.

Symptoms

Upon the parents' leave-taking or homecoming:

1. Crying;
2. Tantrums;
3. Breathholding;
4. Apathy toward the parent or the opposite, frantic clinging.

What to Do

The key to alleviating separation anxiety is to understand the developmental stage that underlies it.

EIGHT MONTHS

1. Bear in mind that your baby's crying will cease after you reappear, even if she has cried the entire time. The reaction

relates to the child's inability to understand constancy—that "out of sight" does not mean "gone forever."

2. Begin to teach independence by having the child play by herself while you are in another room. Reappear frequently; then leave to resume your household or other tasks. Once your baby is used to this procedure, strenuous reactions should decrease.

THIRTEEN MONTHS

1. Try to expose your youngster to other children and adults. The child who has experienced fewer contacts and is "protected" extensively by one parent reacts most strenuously when that parent leaves, even for another room.

2. When away, be specific about the time of your return, and be prompt about this.

EIGHTEEN TO TWENTY-FOUR MONTHS

1. Since a child of this age may grow anxious over changes in locale or routine, avoid major transitions, such as moves or long trips that take you away from home, if you possibly can.

2. If you must travel or use a caretaker, prepare the child by acquainting her with this person *before* you leave. Invite the caretaker to play with your child in your home while you are there, for instance, until they become comfortable with each other.

3. If the child will stay at someone else's house, take the child there for gradually longer periods over a week or two prior to your leaving.

STRANGER ANXIETY: FEAR OF STRANGERS (BIRTH TO THREE YEARS OLD)

Michelle, a new mother, was a thirty-year-old woman who had lived in California away from her family for years. When her sister, Julie, said she was coming to visit, Michelle was ecstatic. She had not seen her sister since before her child's birth six months earlier. Since theirs had always been a close family, Michelle longed to share the new little member with Julie.

When her sister arrived, Michelle ran out to greet her, child in arm. Julie looked at the baby with delight for about three seconds before the little angel emitted a bloodcurdling scream. Despite knowing *something* was wrong, Michelle couldn't find an immediate source for the child's discomfort. Moreover, the baby never ceased screaming until Michelle took her safely away from Julie.

Michelle was now mortified, not comprehending why her daughter would act so horribly before her sister whom she loved so much.

What to do? How do you simultaneously comfort the child while concealing your own embarrassment?

Definition

Like separation anxiety, fear of strangers is a normal phenomenon, indicating that the child is apprehensive about someone she does not know or see regularly. Initially it occurs in the latter half of the child's first year. If a well-fed and diapered baby howls upon someone's entry, stranger anxiety is probably the cause.

During the 1960s two researchers, G. A. Morgan and H. N. Ricciuti, showed that this fear appeared very soon (average of one month) after an infant's first signs of specific attachment to a particular caregiver, usually the mother. Also during this decade, H. R. Schaffer published a study showing that fear of strangers appeared in 69 percent of tested children by the age of thirty-six months, in 94 percent by the age of four years, and in all the subjects eventually. There was, however, a direct correlation between the number of people encountered and the age of stranger anxiety; that is, the greater the number of contacts, the later the onset of fearing strangers. Indeed, studies done following World War II by René Spitz, an English researcher, showed that the only children who exhibited *no* anxiety upon meeting unthreatening strangers were those raised in certain hospitals or orphanages. That is, having lacked close, personal care, they had never formed the sort of attachments that could be threatened by a stranger.

To summarize: No matter how unreasonable such fearful episodes seem to you (knowing that neither your baby-sitter nor your best friend is about to harm your child), they are normal for the developing and loved child.

Symptoms upon the Stranger's Entry

1. Frowning, staring, or wariness;
2. Trembling or stiffening (similar to an animal's "freezing");
3. Crying, with intense emotion;
4. With the older child, hiding behind parent's skirt or legs.

Motivation for Separation Anxiety and Fear of Strangers

If you and your child have endured such scenes, you may not believe the following truths about separation anxiety and fear of strangers. But read on, because each in its way attests to your success at what psychologists call the *infant-parent bonding process.*

During our distant past of both animal and tribal migrations in search of food, safety, and shelter, how long do you think a baby monkey, human, or even goose could have survived if it didn't cling tightly (remember your newborn's intense grasp reflex?) to mother's fur, abdomen, or trail down to the water? Suppose it couldn't differentiate care- and foodgivers from interlopers with strange faces and scents?

Furthermore, and within the caregiver category, according to an interview with pediatrician T. Berry Brazelton, a human infant recognizes and differentiates its mother's or caregiver's smell within the first seven days and her face within fourteen days, and the father's face and smell by fourteen days after birth.

Psychologist and researcher J. Bowlby has spent years identifying the natural stages by which such attachment occurs and what happens if it is disrupted. He concluded that during the first three months an infant is genetically programmed to direct attention toward anyone caring for her. During the second quarter of the first year, the baby begins to focus on one significant person. Months seven through nine intensify this normal attachment, and during the final quarter of the first year the baby completes the attachment by babbling and crying to, or crawling toward and following, this person. That is, such activities intensify with the child's increasing mental and motor abilities.

Thus, separation anxiety, which typically begins between six and ten months, occurs because the infant has begun both to discriminate self from not-self (objects and other humans) and to remember the faces of caregivers. By six to eight months, the baby can hold your image in her mind after you have left the room. Out of sight is no longer out of mind, although the baby who cries upon your leave-taking can often be distracted by someone wielding a new toy. Do you know that the ancient game of peekaboo enchants infants precisely because it repeats disappearance and return under conditions the child can control? As a game, it both reduces anxiety and pleasurizes what in reality can be painful (temporary loss of object).

The older infant experiences forms of separation anxiety related to her developing abilities. At a year to fourteen months the now-mobile toddler fears losing a parent from whom she can already run away, even if only across a room. Twenty to thirty-six months is the usual age for the child to begin outside day care—for many, the first recurrent separation from home and parent.

This age varies, depending on the family work and cultural orientation. When both parents work, or in the case of a single working mother, the age may be younger. The effect of the child leaving in most cases is not problematic. However, this obviously creates a change for the parents as well as the child. Often there is a loss experienced by the primary caretaker when the child goes off to school. Sometimes this is communicated to the child, who then reacts more severely to the separation.

When a child is away from home or parents for a prolonged period through tragedy, such as hospitalization, death, or divorce, such an event no longer involves only separation anxiety but can verge on childhood depression. Although prolonged separations due to family problems cannot always be avoided, it is best to continue as normal a relationship as possible, leaving the child in familiar surroundings. Sometimes it takes an extreme example to demonstrate the wisdom of this. During World War II, for example, many English children were evacuated from the London bombings to safer northern areas. Yet all studies indicated that those separated from parents and familiar neighborhoods became more disturbed than those who stayed with their families through the heavy air raids on London.

To summarize: Every child looks to parents for trust, safety, warmth, and care. Separation anxiety and fear of strangers essentially ensure that access to these normal processes will flow and continue.

What to Do

1. Gradually introduce a new baby-sitter or housekeeper to the child as someone worthy of trust and respect. For example, remain in the room with the new caregiver and the child for some time during the person's first visit. Practice a series of small separations that allow everyone sufficient time to adjust to the new arrangement.

2. Have a new or favorite toy ready for the sitter to use to distract the child when you do leave.

3. Accustom your baby early to a variety of relatives, friends, and other visitors, and to social events outside your home. If possible, take the baby daily to where other small children play. Although yours can't yet join the group's fun, she can either simply watch or play her own game by herself. The point is to accustom the youngster now to the presence of the noisy day-care or play groups he will soon join.

4. For the older child, always state what time you will return from work or other commitment. Point to how far the hands on the clock will move or mention a familiar time mark, such as "After your nap" or "After your dinner."

5. Be sure you arrive back promptly after these first crucial periods away. Letting your sitter as well as the child become anxious only compounds your problem.

6. If tantrums or other distress continues repeatedly upon your leave-taking, examine your own attitudes. Are you somehow conveying to the child your guilt at leaving? Are you overprotective, encouraging the child to cling?

7. Don't punish or spank a grieving child who, after all, is only bemoaning loss of you! Try to make her see that you are dependable, will return, and still love her enough to kiss that tear-smeared face crumpling before you. Resist the temptation to tease or call the child a "sissy," a "baby," or a "coward." Steel yourself, say good-bye cheerfully, and leave, knowing you've done the best you can.

8. Be sure to pack a child's favorite stuffed toy, blanket, pacifier, or other security items when your child embarks on any overnight trip away from home. See also that your baby-sitters know what and where these vital objects are at home.

FEAR OF SUDDEN, LOUD NOISES (FIRST YEAR)

Seven-month-old Susan was a giggly, happy baby, the kind that mothers dream of having. Nevertheless, one day her cooing stopped and she began screaming in her crib. Her mother, Joanna, who was ironing in the next room, ran to help, expecting to find her daughter fallen from the crib.

Nothing was wrong—except that Susan continued to cry inconsolably. After Joanna had picked her up, rocking and soothing her, she began to quiet. Since it was a fine spring day, Joanna pulled the window higher to let in more air.

Just as she returned the baby to the crib, a garbage truck droned and clattered by outside. As it hit a new pothole with a resounding clang, Susan again began to wail.

Symptoms

1. In the younger infant, the startle reflex;
2. Crying that verges on panic upon hearing a loud noise.

Motivation

Fear of loud noises, an innate reflex, is a stage that all children pass through before they understand the nature of machinery and motors, thunder, and so on.

What to Do

1. Hold and comfort the baby to indicate that you can be trusted.
2. Check out sources of noise to which you are accustomed but which may frighten a youngster.
3. If you live in a particularly noisy area, minimize the

child's exposure if possible by providing a back bedroom away from the street.

4. If sudden noises continue to wake or frighten the child, investigate a "white noise" box, sold in some small appliance shops. A round unit that sits on the floor or table, it provides a constant, somewhat hypnotic whir or hiss and masks external sounds. Air conditioners and vaporizers, which have similar sounds, can have a similar effect.

FEAR OF FALLING (FIRST YEAR)

Symptoms

1. Crying and irritability;
2. Struggling to be set down, if held without proper support to head or spine.

Motivation

Fear of falling is both innate and also specific to the way a particular caretaker handles the child. For a humorous comparison, recall how the average toddler picks up a cat—a rough, two-armed lunge to the midsection that leaves the animal's legs and head dangling.

Until six months of age the infant, lying on her back, views the world as a movie at which she is a passive spectator. With the freedom to sit up and crawl comes the active life, which admittedly often conflicts with safety as toddlers proceed to jump off beds, into bathtubs, and down stairways. Realize that the majority of infants, however, *do fear falling* and have shown a surprising awareness of heights in the visual cliff experiment (see Spatial Fear: Heights in Chapter 5).

What to Do

1. Hold the baby as firmly and securely as possible, especially during a bath.

2. If you can't get a good grip on a wiggly baby and it's not a matter of life and death, wait until you're in proper position to pick up the child. This means squarely facing the baby (to prevent wrenching your back muscles) and setting down other objects first.

3. Raise the crib as high as possible for as long as possible (until the child begins to climb out) to minimize the lifting up you must do.

4. For the child learning to crawl, teach her to climb down *backward* (on the belly) from a bed or high place. This will also prevent many stairway accidents.

5. Do everything you can to let the child know that you can be trusted to respond to needs and problems.

BEDTIME AND SLEEP FEARS (APPROXIMATELY SIX MONTHS TO TWENTY-FOUR MONTHS)

Having waited a considerable time to achieve a pregnancy, Tom and Brenda were ecstatic when they discovered that they were having a baby. Although Tommy's arrival thus gave them joy, they were not prepared for his love of the night. A bright, eager baby who never seemed to get enough of life, he always fought going to sleep at night. At six months he would wake in the middle of the night, screaming and inconsolable. Because Brenda couldn't bear his crying, she would run into his room and fetch him into her bed. Lulled by his mother's warmth, he would then drift into quiet sleep. Finally she would carry him back to his crib.

Although Tom was upset by the constant interruptions to their sleep, Brenda thought that this night behavior would abate if she answered it promptly. She was wrong.

Because the pediatrician advised her to let Tommy cry himself back to sleep, she agreed to try this after lengthy soul-searching. And after only three nights Tommy was again sleeping through the dark hours and letting his parents rest, too.

Symptoms

1. Crying at bedtime;
2. Resistance to staying in bed;
3. Dawdling through the bedtime ritual, including, in the older baby, excuses.

Motivation

Like eating, sleep is, of course, one of the areas of a child's life most susceptible to problems. Bedtime fears therefore can occur at all ages for various reasons. Nightly episodes can result from overfatigue or be symptomatic of some other condition or problem, ranging from something physiological, such as getting a cold, to a psychological problem about the parents or home. Common reasons for such problems in normal toddlers may involve separation anxiety (particularly for twelve-, twenty-, and twenty-four-month-old children); nightmares; and illnesses or other physical conditions, such as teething or fear of bed-wetting in the toilet-trained youngster.

It is now known that adults sleep and dream within ninety-minute cycles throughout the night, spending 20 percent of the night in the "fast" REM (rapid eye movement) sleep that produces dreams. By contrast, children have been observed to spend about 50 percent of their sleeptime in the company of such "pictures in my head." As any parent knows, their sleep proceeds like certain small rivers—deep yet restless. The by-now traditional Freudian explanation is that both pleasant dreams and nightmares help vent the "devils of the unconscious," a range of repressed feelings about events that occurred during the day.

It is unfortunate that contemporary cultures, unlike many others in history, seem to ignore the integrative or even prophetic nature of dreams, including children's dreams. The anthropologist K. Stewart described how wisely the Senoi, a Malaysian tribe, react to a child's dream of falling, flying, or climbing when they comment, "That is a wonderful dream, one of the best a man can have. Where did you fall to, and what did you discover?"

Acknowledging, even relaxing into, the alarming material thus converts it from a nightmare into a dream of mastery. This process resembles the various forms of Western psychology, including behavioral therapy, that advocate admitting a problem as the first concrete step toward conquering it.

Current research indicates that sleep patterns are extremely conditionable. Furthermore, the patterns a child develops early will probably form the basis of sleep habits for years into the future. As Brenda, Tom, and their baby discovered, nighttime crying scenes can be avoided by establishing proper sleep habits for the infant as a blessing to all concerned. Here, as with other topics in this book, it is the parents who must lead— difficult and confusing as this is, especially for new parents eager to give their child all possible sympathy and help.

What to Do: Baby's Bedtime

1. Establish proper sleeptime patterns beginning in infancy. For the baby who doesn't yet appreciate adult distinctions between day and night, make night feedings and changings brief and dimly lit. For the baby who is fussing, try whatever it takes—short of habituating the baby to your bed or bribing with bottles of milk or juice pressed against new teeth.

2. If rocking helps, buy a set of rocker springs that temporarily replace the wheels or rollers on the crib.

3. Blanket holders (plastic garterlike devices that attach to crib bars) will keep the nighttime covers on an active baby. Place them under the crib bumpers, away from the child's fingers or mouth.

4. Learn to differentiate between the infant crying from hunger and one crying for attention. The young child will very quickly get used to the extra attention of a parent rocking the child, staying up with her, or placing her in the parents' bed.

WHAT TO DO—FOR YOUNG INFANTS

1. After the child wakes for a feeding and finishes, place her back in her crib. If crying persists which is clearly not related to hunger or wetness, let the child cry herself to sleep. This is hard to do, but in the long run better for the child as well as the parents.

2. For the older infant, begin a fifteen-minute bedtime ritual of whatever activities you both enjoy. These may include a quick bath; making a game of picking up toys; a song, story, or any quiet activity during which the child has your undivided attention. Sometimes saying "Good night, room. Good night, woolly bear. Good night, arms. Good night (whatever)" has a soothing, hypnotic effect.

At the end of the allotted period, *leave* the room knowing that you have done your job and the baby must do the rest.

3. To avoid interruptions that can prolong the bedtime process, take your phone off the hook if necessary and try to keep older children occupied and away from baby's room.

4. Encourage use of transitional objects, such as a soft towel or stuffed bear that the child can hug. Make the finding of these items a part of straightening the room each evening.

5. If the baby's windows face east or south into the sun, consider using blackout shades or lengths of black cloth to drape the window frames.

6. If you desire an infant or toddler to fall asleep promptly in the evening, do not let an afternoon nap stretch toward dinnertime. Wake the child up even though she may strenuously resist and this may complicate your return from work or dinner preparations.

7. Do not fear to let a healthy infant of six or more months cry for five or ten minutes at bedtime or during the night. Investigate only if it goes on longer. Remember, however, that separation anxiety does peak at approximately eight, thirteen, twenty, and twenty-four months.

WHAT TO DO: TODDLER'S BEDTIME

1. If the young child develops a sleep disturbance, consult first with your pediatrician to rule out any physical reason for the reaction. Assuming no illness, this is a pattern that can easily be broken. The remedy often involves letting the child cry until she falls asleep. Usually a regimen of letting the child cry causes three or four nights of difficulty for parents but results in the child finally sleeping through the night. If a child cries twenty to thirty minutes on the first night, this should decrease to ten or twenty on the second night, and a manageable five to ten on the third. Before the end of a week the child should be going to sleep without incident.

2. If a child becomes ill or experiences a change in routine because of a trip or for some other reason, expect a regression to an earlier pattern and reassert the above training.

3. Continue the bedtime ritual of tasks. Name and do them with the child at first, but make her increasingly responsible for performing them in the same order nightly while you watch or supervise. A sample routine may be to start undressing; get into pajamas; use the toilet (if child is toilet-trained); brush teeth; and pick up toys—for completion of which the reward is the child's choice of story or game.

4. To avoid interruptions that can sabotage your efforts, see number 3 regarding baby's bedtime.

5. If your almost toilet-trained child worries about bed-wetting, continue with night diapers and waterproof pads and assure her you love her anyway. To help her keep dry, ask the last person who goes to bed at night to take the toddler to the bathroom or potty.

6. If you have an active child who never seems tired, even at the end of the bedtime ritual, insist on a quiet time alone in bed with words like, "You can play for fifteen minutes with the light on, but you have to stay in bed." Then return at the time you've stated.

7. To avoid a wearying succession of bedtime drinks, snacks, and toilet requests, remind the child that she just had whatever it is. Say a pleasant but firm good night; turn out the light; and *leave* immediately. If the child is well and healthy, do not allow yourself to be detained or to look hesitant or worried.

8. If a child later wanders out to join your evening activity or enter your bed, carry or walk her *silently* back to her own room. This seems nearly impossible to do at first, but it is the only way to return her to bed without encouraging her bid for attention.

9. Besides the ill child referred to in number 2 above, the other exception is the child who rouses you because she is only half-awake but screaming from a nightmare. Massage or hug the child, identify the experience for the child as a nightmare, and encourage her to tell you about it. Use words such as, "Did you have a scary dream? What happened? Tell me about it. You're okay now." No matter how creative or fanciful the tale, be sure not to ridicule or criticize. Remember that nightmares are rarely staged to get your attention.

10. If bedtime or sleep disturbances persist, reconsider the amount and quality of the child's nutrition, especially at the evening meal. A new specialty called *orthomolecular medicine* investigates the relationship among diet, illness, and behavior, especially the presence of previously unsuspected allergies to common staples of a child's diet, such as wheat, milk, and citrus foods. Serving regular, balanced meals does much to minimize the irritability, negativity, and overfatigue caused by an empty stomach—and the accompanying need to snack on cookies and candy.

The fear of sleeping is not so important here as what to do about it. Most children of this age are highly conditionable. Establishing a good bedtime routine to encourage sleep is paramount, since bad sleep routines quickly become habits which are very hard to change later.

We can see from this discussion that fear may be but one reason for sleep problems. What is important for you as the parent is to be able to identify the source of the problem and deal with it in the appropriate manner. The child who is staying up to exert her independence and power needs to be dealt with differently from the child who is suddenly afraid of the dark.

FEAR OF ANIMALS (BIRTH TO THREE YEARS OLD)

Thirteen-month-old Benjamin was taking his first steps, and his parents were rightly proud. Wherever they went, they walked with him half-suspended between them while he giggled and toddled along.

One day as they visited a friend's house, the resident black tomcat—aptly named Monster—walked over to sniff and investigate Benjamin. Monster's childrenless owners hadn't thought to exile the cat outside during the visit. At first Benjamin stared awestruck at this creature with its plume of a tail that twitched higher than the boy's head. Shrieking with delight, he then rushed the cat, ready to hug this warm, living version of his stuffed animals. He began by grabbing Monster's "handle"—the now violently twitching tail.

Monster, which had initially tolerated Benjamin, suddenly decided to end the relationship. Having growled and twisted around to free his tail, he spat at Benjamin.

The boy's face registered amazement, shock, and finally total terror. Next he emitted a yelp that announced his plight to the entire neighborhood. Even Benjamin's mother couldn't comfort him for some time.

For months afterward, he screamed at the sight of a cat.

Definition

This fear, which under such conditions is perfectly normal, results from an animal experience that, by exposing the child's extreme vulnerability, produces an intense reaction.

Symptoms

1. Stiffening of the child's body;
2. Crying;
3. Trembling;
4. Clinging to an adult.

Motivation

Fear of animals usually begins after a child is six months old. According to Isaac Marks' *Fears and Phobias,* it represents or consolidates three basic or innate fears of infants: the fears of sudden motion, loud or abrupt noise, and sudden, close approach. The child isn't afraid of the danger as much as these other factors.

What to Do

1. Know that this specific fear is usually outgrown. Be sure, however, that it is not due to an animal bite, which may require professional or medical attention.

2. If you feel comfortable with domestic pets, but have none of your own, find situations where the child can play with animals and learn to treat them properly.

3. Never leave a baby or toddler alone with a bottle of milk and a pet, no matter how reliable or tame the animal seems. Feed older toddlers away from the animal, and instruct them not to "share" with the dog or cat at the table or anywhere else.

4. If your child continues to fear animals, examine your own attitudes. An infant's fear can occur in response to parental fear that the child intuits and models.

TYPICAL FEARS DURING THE SECOND YEAR
(TWELVE TO TWENTY-FOUR MONTHS)

During these months a child can acquire fear of the dark, thunder and lightning, the bath, and toilet training. Fears of separation, strangers, animals, and the pediatrician can continue. Discipline, if inconsistent, can confuse and worry a child.

FEARS ABOUT INCONSISTENT DISCIPLINE
(SECOND YEAR)

Symptoms

1. Irritability, nervousness, demandingness;
2. Cringing, if expecting discipline when an adult approaches.

Motivation

Maintaining consistent expectations and standards while also cooperating with a growing child's demands is one of parenthood's most intense challenges. Yet discipline becomes crucial to the child's sense of security. Children, having learned the power of a healthy scream, next become most "persuasive" at getting parents to do what they want. Unfortunately, this power is rarely used with wisdom or judgment but only to gratify immediate wishes.

A child's behavior becomes only more difficult when a parent can't or won't maintain consistency, although this is often hard to do, given the trials and tension of daily life.

The task combines setting standards that a child can follow without dawdling or defeat and that a parent can maintain without shouting or hitting. As much as parents aim to be cooperative and pleasant, it is difficult not to lash out at a toddler who has ignored the first—or second—warning not to touch the stereo set or the china closet and has just entered forbidden territory. Although a shouting rampage helps the parent vent anger, it frightens the child, decreasing the sense of security by making the reactions seem capricious or unpredictable. And since a violent response may or may not occur, the child's already innate resolve to do what she pleases may be strengthened.

What to Do

1. Remember that the child at this age has just begun to realize that she is a person both mobile and separate from the caretaker.

2. Remember that the child acts most often in the heat or spur of the moment—not with malice aforethought.

3. Monitor your reactions and avoid excessive outbursts. As an adult, you should be able to do this even when you are tired or busy. Firmly remove the child's hands from a forbidden object, rather than striking out or screaming.

4. When frustrated by a child's ignoring of your requests, try to find a creative way to gain cooperation. This may involve distraction with a toy, patient questioning, or (for the older child) some kind of trade of goods or services so that you both attain what you want.

5. Sort out your own feelings about discipline and family or household standards. Having decided what really matters to you and what you can ignore for a while, be as consistent as possible on those tasks or needs that really matter to you.

6. If you and your spouse don't agree on acceptable behavior for the child or yourselves as parents, work it out together first. See further suggestions in Chapter 11.

DOWN THE DRAIN: ANNIHILATION, ESPECIALLY BATHROOM FEARS (FIRST AND SECOND YEARS)

Monique, two years old, didn't always hate her bathtime. As an infant, her mother had taken her into her own bath, where they had a fine time laughing and playing. Until the moment for hairwashing arrived, Monique always played happily with her toys. Although she never enjoyed hairwashing, its discomfort did pass quickly.

Suddenly, however, around her second birthday, Monique

began to object whenever her mother said, "It's bathtime." At first, Monique said "No!" and soon escalated to a full tantrum.

Not understanding the change, her mother feared that bathing would involve incessant difficulty.

Her pediatrician helped the situation by explaining the fear that occasionally develops around two years of age—that the baby will go out with the bathwater. A small child, seeing the water vanish down the drain, concludes that this can happen to her, too.

Although most children enjoy the splashing and soothing that warm water can provide, occasionally a youngster, even one who has never been injured in the bathroom, will begin to fear events there in both bathtub and toilet.

Symptoms

1. Crying and other negative behavior, including tantrums;
2. Becoming rigid when confronted with the bath or a flushing toilet.

Motivation

At about the age of two, the child first begins to understand the powerful principle of cause and effect—along with an equally strong and frustrating sense of how much of the world she cannot control. To compensate, the child begins to fantasize about, and believe in, magic "to get what I want," as one boy said. Desires about flying (by flapping arms), avoiding a scolding (by vanishing or shrinking to doll size), or multiplying strength (by wearing a special Skeletor or Superman shirt) are examples of the useful side of magic's power.

Its dark side begets in some children the fear of *involuntarily* disappearing inside the vacuum cleaner or down the drain with the water in the bath or toilet. For many, the radical separation between self and others, between self and what to adults are powerless, depersonalized things, has not yet fully dawned. If the vacuum cleaner sounds mad at me, why shouldn't it want to suck me in? is a common fantasy.

Moreover, certain youngsters are particularly sensitive to even the most mundane changes, such as ending a favorite activity or beginning to undress for a bath. Child psychiatrist Stella Chess has termed them "temperamentally difficult" and recognized two of their qualities as oversensitivity to sound or touch (as in bathing) and difficulty with transitions (as at bedtime). Such extreme reactions stem from a basic temperament that has, of course, been present since birth in a personality that Dr. Chess calls "a difficult child." And these reactions do differ from the normal developmental fears of most children. If your child has such symptoms as difficulty with transitions, irregular eating or sleeping, hyperactivity, hypersensitivity to touch or sound, or high intensity level, refer to Dr. Chess' work on the "difficult child" or Stanley Turecki's *The Difficult Child.*

What to Do

We assume that you have followed such sensible infant bathing tips as the following:

1. Cushion a slippery baby on a large sponge or foam pillow placed in sink or tub, making sure that her head is well supported.

2. For the baby or toddler who objects to being totally undressed, compromise with a sponge bath of the top half first, followed by partially redressing her and sponging the bottom half.

3. Take the baby into the bath with you and rest her securely between your legs.

4. Remove an infant from the water and lay her securely on a towel on the floor *before* you pull the stopper or plug in the bathtub.

A couple of shampooing tips:

1. Use a "football hold," with the baby's head cradled in your left hand, legs tucked under your left arm. Your right arm (assuming you're right-handed) is now free for washing.

2. Similarly, lean a child's head *backward* (beauty-parlor style) into the basin or tub. This keeps suds well away from the eyes.

Tips for handling the toddler who is already water-resistive:

1. Try to interest her in mixing a special bubble bath or floating a new toy or duck. Any novel or amusing distraction often eases a difficult situation.

2. Reassure the child that she cannot possibly swirl down a drainhole smaller than even an infant's fist.

3. Show pictures of fish, submarines, and other entities that require water to live or function. Or take her to a pet shop to see a nonthreatening aquarium.

4. Reward the bath-fearful child who has just washed successfully. Use verbal praise, handclapping, or whatever she enjoys.

5. *Never* throw a child into water as a quick way to teach swimming, since this will trigger an automatic flailing for survival and can be traumatic.

6. Consider that, according to many pediatricians, any child not yet independent enough to play outside in the dirt doesn't need a daily bath, particularly in winter, when dry skin can be a problem. Do you know that many hospital nurseries cleanse just "top and tail"—those two crucial ends of a newborn?

MEDICAL FEARS (ONE TO THREE YEARS OLD)

Irene was a lovely sixteen-month-old girl who had always been friendly and lovable. Indeed, her mother considered her a nearly perfect child. Knowing she could depend on Irene's good behavior, she eagerly showed the child off to people, including the pediatrician, who had been a family friend for years.

During previous visits to the doctor, Irene had always behaved well. On one occasion, therefore, she had been playing quietly and talking happily to herself before the doctor entered the examining room. As the doctor approached now, however, she became rigid. Next she screwed up her face and emitted a wail that sounded as if someone had stepped on her foot.

Her mother flushed and became exceedingly embarrassed, worrying that the pediatrician would interpret Irene's terrified exterior as the way the child truly felt about him.

Looking at both mother and daughter with empathy, the pediatrician merely announced that the visits would be like this until Irene turned three years of age.

Definition of Medical Fear

For this youngest age group, medical fears, when present, are usually shown in the pediatrician's office or at the hospital, particularly if surgery and its attendant tests become necessary. Between the ages of one and three, negative reactions to pediatricians and their assistants are common and partly caused by stranger anxiety. That is, a child who went willingly to the doctor's office, where she has just waited and played happily, now tenses or screams upon the entry of the doctor—a stranger who is, after all, being probing and personal. Such fear is normal for this age.

To the parent's embarrassment, however, neither exhortations nor encouragements seem to ease the youngster. Distraction with a favorite toy or by a talented pediatrician is the key to calming the child. One doctor we know has perfected a range of birdcalls and mouth clicks he saves especially for the child's ear as he deftly continues his exam. Even a wailing child is so curious that she stops for a few seconds to stare around. Another clever pediatrician trusts the child to handle his shiny instruments—otoscope or stethoscope—first before he uses them. He then lets the child "blow out" the light, for instance, and play with tongue depressors or a latex glove.

In this age group a more serious fear of doctors is related to specific, negative experiences that a hospitalized or very ill child may have experienced during extensive medical testing, complete with needle pricks and blood sampling. Help for this trauma involves allowing the child to play out such conflicts; see suggestions 6 and 7 (under What to Do) below.

Symptoms of Medical Fear

1. Rigidity upon doctor's or assistant's entry;
2. Crying or negative behavior of various kinds, such as saying "The doctor's mean and yucky."

Motivation

For this age group (one to three years), the most common cause is stranger anxiety. Another cause is restlessness and tension from waiting while hearing the wails of other children. The ideal pediatrician's office has plenty of toys, sufficient secretarial help, and a calm, happy atmosphere—and follows appointment times.

What to Do

1. Although most pediatricians know how to handle this fear, discuss the office visit with the child ahead of time, if

possible. You can get a plastic doctor's kit to demonstrate the use of stethoscope, tongue depressor, and ear and eye tools. Say something like, "The doctor will look at you and try to figure out what's wrong so you can feel better really fast."

2. To occupy both of you during possible office waits, bring a book, toy, bottle, or pacifier—whatever it takes to keep your youngster busy and happy.

3. If you have an agreeable doctor, ask him or her to "examine" first the child's doll or stuffed toy.

4. Don't discuss your own medical or dental fears with a child.

5. Don't threaten a child with illness, such as, "If you don't eat, you'll get sick."

6. Mr. Rogers' *Going to the Doctor* is a great book to help explain doctor's visits to young children.

7. For the youngster who needs surgery or other hospital treatment, a good basic book is *The Sad Sick Squirrel Gets Well* by Bruce Camille (Creative Learning Service, 102 Grenoble Place, Hoptacong, NJ 07843).

Inquire whether your hospital has any audiovisual materials to educate children about operations and hospital procedures. Studies from the 1970s showed that children facing surgery for hernia, tonsillectomy, and urogenital difficulties who viewed a film of a child hospitalized and recovering were much less anxious both before and after the operation (three to four weeks). According to their parents, they also exhibited fewer behavior problems compared with similar children facing surgery who saw an unrelated film.

Excellent material is available from Project Health PACT (Participatory and Assertive Consumer Training, University of Colorado Health Sciences Center, C-287, 42 East 9th Avenue, Denver, CO 80262). Encompassing various items from comic books and film strips to school lesson plans, it is graded by ages and designed to alleviate the following unfortunately typical situation. When PACT asked children across the country to illustrate "what you do when you go to the doctor, feelings of inferiority and intimidation poured from every crayon." PACT teaches children to "talk, listen, learn, ask questions, help make decisions, and follow up on health recommendations when they go to any kind of health center."

Although such skills are beyond your toddler, they should not be beyond you if you have a reasonably agreeable and empathetic doctor. For instance, asking your pediatrician to draw a simple picture of what is wrong or painful in the child's body or how a medicine is supposed to work can often embolden or equip you with enough information to discuss the matter afterward with your child. Ask the doctor to decelerate and explain unfamiliar terminology or phraseology.

8. Many hospitals now have facilities to help children cope psychologically with chronic or acute illness requiring lengthy convalescence. One, the Child Life Program at the University of California, Irvine Medical Center, treats babies and toddlers recovering from such traumas as burns, broken bones, and cancer surgery. The children can use the activities room and enjoy both the special staff and the chance to express their conflicts through creative play and artwork of various kinds. "It's a sort of haven for them in here," remarked one volunteer. "It helps them forget they're sick." And pediatrics nurse Sue Ahearn praised therapist Carolyn Spungin, who heads the program, by saying, "She interacts with the children in a nonthreatening way. She doesn't wear a uniform. She doesn't give shots. She doesn't put in an IV. She doesn't cause pain. So the children turn to Carolyn because she's not threatening."

Although everyone entering a hospital needs reassurance, children separated from home and parents certainly can profit from these specially staffed programs.

TYPICAL FEARS DURING THE THIRD YEAR
(TWENTY-FOUR TO THIRTY-SIX MONTHS)

The child's development to age three is incredible. The infant, who began by relating only to breast or bottle, develops into a functioning being with a personality, including abilities to think and talk.

Although a child now walks and talks like a miniature adult, a parent should remember that she really is not— yet. That is, the world still looms large; tasks are difficult, although mastery of them (even figuring out how to screw and unscrew a jar lid) occasions great joy. As a parent, try primarily to *understand* your child's fears, including how the world looks from two feet high, rather than merely reacting to or against them.

The fears of the third year thus parallel a child's development. Children of this age are learning many skills—interaction with peers and parents, control of body functions, and testing of new powers, including imaginative play techniques and energetic use of the word "No!" Attaining these skills coincides with considerable increase in the number of a child's fears. Although the "terrible twos" are normally viewed as an attempt by the child to assert her will on the world, some of a child's poor behavior can be in response to fears.

Fear of animals, separation, strangers, and toilet training may persist, while fresh fears can involve drains (annihilation) and new situations. Objects of fear can change rapidly and mysteriously from day to day.

FEARS ABOUT TOILET TRAINING
(SECOND AND THIRD YEARS)

Except for a bout with colic, twenty-month-old Ian had always been a good child, which included taking down his diaper and using the potty by himself one day. Since his mother believed this action proved how bright he was, she grew ecstatic—not the least because she also hated changing diapers.

She now began toilet training Ian. Following all the books, she praised him, gave him fruit bits, and did everything else to help him learn the potty habit.

At first Ian had accidents frequently. Next his behavior began to deteriorate until he was irritable, waking frequently at night and refusing foods he normally ate. Since his behavior remained within the range of the merely annoying, his mother didn't connect it with the stress of toilet training.

One day a friend suggested putting him back in diapers because she had faced a similar situation. When she did this, the behavior subsided.

Symptoms of Premature Training

1. Irritable behavior;
2. Sudden mood changes;
3. Waking at night.

Motivation

As the child matures, various fears arise because of, or around, the issue of toilet training. If training occurs too early, responses like Ian's can develop. The older child can fear soiling, bed-wetting, or the toilet itself (see Fear of Bedwetting in Chapter 3).

Toilet training is often a charged topic for both parent and child. Most parents attach a value to it that exceeds the actual act, which is no more than achieving muscular control. Some children do this earlier than others, but this ability never correlates to intelligence.

The parent's positive reaction delights the child who is just learning such control. After all, when else can a two-year-old get a grown adult to jump up and down and applaud? Muscular control, of course, brings not only power but stress and anxiety, since failure involves parental disappointment.

Before you despair, remember your child can't be the only one on the street in danger of marrying in a white lace diaper! Know that when it is time, the miracle will occur, and your child, too, will be trained.

What to Do

1. If a child's general behavior changes suddenly at the time of training or other stress, look for the connection.

2. Be tolerant and appreciative of the child's efforts, however inadequate.

3. Praise the child for any successes.

4. Let the child occasionally observe older children of the same sex using the toilet properly.

5. Follow the guides to healthy toilet training, such as *Toilet Training in Less Than a Day* by Nathan Azrin and Richard M. Fox.

HEIGHTENED FEAR RESPONSE DURING THIRD YEAR (TWENTY-FOUR TO THIRTY-SIX MONTHS)

Because Amelia seemed always so placid, her mother, Mary, was startled to watch the little girl, now nearly three, shrink and grow timid in both familiar and new situations. Whereas previously Amelia, like a friendly puppy, had rushed up to strangers in the playground, street, or market, now she hung back, whimpering, "I'm scared, Mommy. That lady scared me" or crying, "That dog wants to eat me." The "lady" and the "dog" in question, of course, were a tiny, arthritic woman hobbling above her cane and a dejected hound down the street that cringed if you only looked at him.

No longer cute, Amelia's worries, which included every cartoon character with teeth, had become a nuisance that required attention both at home and outdoors. The girl's mother, who had hoped for an easier life once babyhood and toilet training were over, now found she could no longer cope alone in public with Amelia's tears and hanging back. Her husband felt that Mary must be doing something wrong, so asking her husband to come on every outing produced tension and complaints from him. Amelia's mother was stymied.

Symptoms

1. Sudden show of fear in situations where previously a child seemed at ease;
2. Inconstancy of fear objects from day to day;
3. Crying, clinging, or negativity.

Motivation

At two-and-a-half to three a child becomes capable of imaginative play. Since the mind plays tricks as well as games, the child feels fear from both actual situations and the imaginary ones she constructs.

What to Do

1. Continue whatever you usually do, such as hugging, stroking, distraction, and so forth, to help your child feel secure.

2. Don't belittle the new or current fear, but don't overdo attention to the fantasy aspect of it, either.

3. Identify for the child that this is fear, and clarify why the child is afraid. "That's a lady whose back hurts because she's bent over. She won't hurt anybody. And I certainly won't let anything bad happen to you."

4. Realize that many of these fears, although melodramatic and embarrassing, are serious to the child and transient.

5. If, however, a particular fear doesn't pass or the child's reactions become more extreme, seek your pediatrician's help.

CHAPTER 3

. . .

Good Night, Cookie Monster: Fears of Three- to Six-Year-Olds

TYPICAL FEARS OF THREE-YEAR-OLDS

With their now active imaginations working inside a widened fantasy life, children of this age are a relatively fearful group who can also be troubled by the inconsistency of their fears. The parent may notice, for instance, that a neighborhood dog, dreaded one week, will be smiled at the next by the same child.

Common fears involve new situations, the dark, dogs, scary noises (especially fire engines), monsters on TV, and first worries about death. Problems around feeding or toilet training can intensify fears in these areas for the child who is "almost" toilet trained.

TYPICAL FEARS OF FOUR-YEAR-OLDS
These youngsters continue to fear the dark, animals, monsters, and new situations, including day care. New fears involve bad thoughts and loss of control, both related to Oedipal issues, desire for aggression, and imagined loss of a parent.

TYPICAL FEARS OF FIVE-YEAR-OLDS
Children of this age usually experience fewer fears—and those more based in reality—than the monsters and ghosts that can plague a four-year-old. Some fears, which can begin at five and intensify at five-and-a-half, involve dogs; sounds (auditory fear), such as thunder, static, or ugly voices; and spaces (getting lost).

The prime fear, however, remains (as at four) the possibility of losing mother or the caretaking parent.

FEARS OF THE DARK AND BEDTIME

It was 3 A.M. in the quiet suburban village where Henry and Janet lived. Their two children—four-year-old Susan and ten-year-old Seth—also were sleeping soundly, and everything seemed peaceful enough. When a cat meowing near Susan's window awakened her, however, she stared around her room and began screaming. When her startled mother entered, Susan only screamed louder. Indeed, nothing calmed her until the light was on, and her mother was hugging her tightly.

Definition

Fear of the dark occurs when a child either wakes up at night or is required to stay in darkness at bedtime.

Symptoms

1. Various exhibitions of intense discomfort, such as crying, calling out, or protesting ("Don't wanna sleep!");
2. Anxiety reactions, including rapid heartbeat or breathing;
3. Leaving bed to search out parents.

Motivation

Assuming that neither nightmares nor imaginary monsters are troubling your child, the usual cause for fear of the dark is the loss of control that happens when familiar furnishings and people seem absent within the night's blackness. One area of development that occurs between ages three and six is the child's ability to "organize" the world. Defenses are developed to ward off anxiety, and the child learns means to keep realities in perspective. Specific abilities allow the child to identify and differentiate reality from fantasy, organize thoughts and drives for effective functioning, and reject frightening thoughts.

However, all these noble aims can suffer or retreat in the presence of darkness and shadow. The child becomes most easily disoriented at night or upon waking from deep sleep into a world of shadows, animal sounds, rattling windows, banging radiators, or creaking floorboards, all exaggerated by darkness, even in the quietest houses or apartments.

At the age of four, the fear of abandonment—more related to separation anxiety—also peaks. The normal four- or five-year-old, therefore, may awaken and become confused and panicky. At this age, abandonment means definitive separation from the loved parent, plus a sense that such separation is total and final.

At ages five and six, the child's awareness of sexuality also dawns, and the Oedipal complex described so elegantly by Freud emerges. Now the child wants to be with the opposite-sex parent exclusively. A little girl will tell her father her serious plan to have Mommy leave and to marry Daddy.

Few children, however, can even imagine this without fearing recrimination from the rejected parent. Moreover, the loneliness of a dark room can enhance such fears until the child fears the dark itself as well.

Of course, problems at bedtime occur or recur for other reasons, too, such as illness, fear of nightmares or of bed-wetting, or stress from parental or school problems. Although they resemble the toddler's sleep problems, the motivation is probably different, given the child's increasing maturity.

It is curious that primeval fears of things like the dark, nighttime abandonment, monsters, and rarely encountered animals, such as snakes or lions, have survived into our brightly lit and heavily populated contemporary society. Not wolves, but German shepherds, not tigers but housecats, are the animals that share our children's environment. Moreover, it is a rare parent today who intentionally frightens children with tales of ghosts, witches, hell, devils, or bears in the local woods in order to ensure obedience and docility.

One psychologist and theorist, Carl Jung, hypothesized that we all share a "collective unconscious" that stores memories genetically transmitted from our earliest ancestors, from a time when humans were a fragile species fighting fierce beasts for survival in the jungle or plains. In this context, some of the fearful responses and even the fears of the modern child recall a prototypical world still alive inside us.

What to Do

1. After turning out the main light in your child's room, identify for him the new appearance of familiar objects. "Do you see your teddy bear, your fish tank, your pillow?"

2. Use a night-light placed where it will not augment the shadows.

3. Leave the child's door ajar and assure him you will remain nearby.

4. If your child wakes crying in the night for no reason you can discover, go in to reassure him with comforting words such as "I know it's scary because it's dark." Then reorient the child by saying, "But there's your Moosie doll and the chair with your clothes."

5. Don't, however, habituate the child to a nightly visit, since parental attention in the wee hours can be habit-forming. Insist that the night-light should help him feel grown up enough to sleep without you.

6. The next day, reward the child for nights that pass quietly without sleep problems. Problem nights should go unremarked.

7. If the child's sleep disturbance persists for longer than one week, see the previous section on helping the child learn better sleeping patterns.

8. If sleep disturbances are due to some stressful period of illness or family difficulty, try honestly to identify the cause and do what you can to minimize pressure upon the child. Although it may seem nearly impossible to empathize with a youngster's viewpoint at a time when you're burdened with your own worries, it is worth the effort in the end. And you will regain the sleep you badly need.

FEAR OF MONSTERS, GHOSTS, WITCHES, AND OTHER CREATURES

William at four was an adorable boy who lived in a large New York apartment with two brothers, his mother, and father. One night everyone was awakened by a shriek: "Daddy, come quick!"

William's father leapt from his bed with the agility only fear for one's child can bestow. Racing to his son's room, he found the boy shuddering and crying. "Daddy, there's a monster in here. I saw it. He had giant teeth and blue eyes. He wants to eat me and then everybody."

The terror was real.

His father answered, "If there's a monster here, he better clear out or I'll get him." Picking up a yellow plastic baseball bat, he swung furiously into every corner of the room and toward the ceiling.

"It's safe now," he announced.

The boy went to sleep.

Definition

This fear of imaginary entities manifests when a child feels both vulnerable (as at night) and worried about physical injury to self or others from superhuman creatures.

Symptoms

1. Reluctance when going alone into dark rooms or outdoors at night;
2. Covering eyes or shrinking into chair during terrifying television or film shows, including cartoons.

Motivation

Monsters of all varieties and dimensions are projections of a child's worst fears at a time when he may be frightened from both outside and inside. These private and visiting "demons" may be considered the child's way to formalize and project onto the outside world whatever internal feelings of anger, hatred, or desire for revenge have become stressful.

Before the contemporary era of mass media, children saw species of monsters in puppet shows and other plays and heard of them nightly in literature's oldest forms, myths and fairy tales. Such tales have always dealt with humanity's most troublesome questions of good, evil, justice, death, thirst for adventure, and hope for the future, including every child's dream that even the poorest and meekest—Jack and his mother at the foot of the beanstalk, for instance—may live and prosper.

In *The Uses of Enchantment,* psychologist Bruno Bettelheim describes why these tales have endured the centuries:

> It is characteristic of fairy tales to state an existential dilemma briefly and pointedly: the need to be loved and the fear that one is thought worthless, the love of life, and the fear of death. . . .
>
> Modern stories written for young children mainly avoid these existential problems. . . . There is a widespread refusal to let children know that the source of much that goes wrong in life is due to our very own natures—the propensity of all men for acting aggressively, asocially, selfishly, out of anger and anxiety. Instead, we want our children to believe that, inherently, all men are good. But children know that they are not always good; and often, even when they are, they would prefer not to be. This contradicts what they are told by their parents, and therefore makes the child a monster in his own eyes.

[Thus] . . . the child fails to get to know his monster better, nor is he given suggestions as to how he may gain mastery over it. As a result, the child remains helpless with his worst anxieties—much more so than if he had been told fairy tales which give these anxieties form and body and also show ways to overcome these monsters. If our fear of being devoured takes the tangible form of a witch, it can be gotten rid of by burning her in the oven!

Obviously this book does not advocate witch burning or cannibalism. The point is the *process* by which Hansel and, even more, Gretel, forced to leave home, used their wits to avoid death, conquer their enemy, and return richer and wiser to presumably stunned parents.

What to Do

1. Remember that one or more monsters are part of every child's normal mental life at this age. Failure to discriminate reality from fantasy, plus your child's normal egocentricity, also ensure that any available wandering monsters must be pursuing him personally.

2. If your child seems easily frightened or prone to let the monsters disrupt daytime life, begin by restricting television to programs with little monster or horror content. The Nickelodeon cable TV channel, for one, has delightful cartoons of prizewinning artistic quality. "Sesame Street" and the Muppets have done a great service by making monsters so bumbling or comical that they become friendly.

By contrast to often worrisome TV, a fairy tale read by a trusted person resembles a game of peekaboo. The child can get immediate answers to questions or end the fairy tale easily if he wants.

3. If your child awakens at night troubled by a ghost or other imaginary creature, use the reorienting technique described in Fears of the Dark and Bedtime.

4. If a certain monster persists, have the child draw its picture as one way of befriending it. Discuss the drawing with the child.

5. Then, don't stress the object of the fear but the child's ability to overcome it. Depending on the monster's locale and habits, examine inside the closet or under the bed in the evening; turn the dresser mirror away from the child's view; spray the room with an empty aerosol can; beat the air with a broomstick.

Teach the child antifear statements such as, "I'm a big boy. I can beat that ghost." "That creep won't scare me unless I let him."

6. If the child resists these statements, try making friends with the monster by stressing, for instance, how lonely it must be to come only at night when nobody's around and that the monster is probably so ugly no one can stand to see it, and so on. The rationale for this is that it's hard to fear something you have begun to pity.

7. No matter how unrealistic the resident monster, do not ridicule his creator, the child, nor belittle the fear by calling it "silly."

8. Fears can be related to traumatic experiences. Never lock a small child into a closet, car, cellar, or other dark, solitary place as a disciplinary measure. Standing alone in a quiet corner of the room is sufficiently boring discipline for the average youngster.

Make sure that other disciplinary techniques fit the misdeed. Here is one that obviously didn't: When the filmmaker Alfred Hitchcock was five years old and had committed some minor transgression, his father sent him to the local police station with a note. Having read it, the officer in charge locked Alfred into a cell, saying, "This is what we do to bad boys." Although he was released a mere five minutes later, he never forgot the sense of total abandonment. The terror of arrest and confinement recurs often in his films—an eloquent reminder to parents that discipline of small children should be appropriate, never destroying their ability to cope.

9. Do not use going to bed as a threat or punishment.

FEAR OF ANIMALS

Four-year-old Marianna was playing in the park when her mother saw a huge St. Bernard dog approaching. Still a rollicking puppy, the dog was friendly enough—but twice Marianna's size—as he sniffed about her and wagged his broom of a tail. Marianna ran screaming to her mother.

For two months afterward, the sight of any dog, large or small, threw her into a fit of clinging and crying.

Definition and Symptoms

Although fears of animals persist throughout childhood, each age group exhibits characteristic behavior when confronting such a problem. A four-year-old, for instance, shows distress by crying or freezing when encountering (or contemplating encountering) the animal. At times the fear may also generalize to fears of other animals.

Motivation

Fear of animals is one of several areas in children's lives where it becomes necessary to distinguish a normal, self-protective reaction from that caused by trauma (see below) or by modeling an adult's panic upon seeing some creeping insect or rodent.

To many children, animals—whether liked or disliked—

become as, or even more, important than people. Parents and teachers are busy adults who work or otherwise may not always be available. By contrast, many family pets enjoy cuddling while the child watches television or sleeps, and caged pets are always available. Children therefore easily attribute to animals an unrealistic range of emotions and intelligence. Moreover, young children are fascinated with animal attributes, such as power, size, equipment (claws, fangs), and ability (flying, galloping).

As with monsters, the negative side emerges whenever children feel powerless upon confronting one of these seemingly perfected creatures, even if it's a chihuahua with a bark no bigger than its mouth.

No matter how the animal question is asked from study to study, researchers discover two salient facts: (1) fear of animals affects the majority of children, and (2) it decreases sharply with age. One researcher who has published many articles on normal children's responses to animals is Adah Maurer of the University of California, Berkeley. Here are sample results from one of his studies. As part of the Wechsler Intelligence test, 112 children, aged five to twelve, were asked, "What are things to be afraid of?"

Of the 467 responses, 233 or 50 percent, consisted of a single category: animals. . . . The most unpopular animal is the snake. . . . Next in order come lions, tigers, and bears.

Eighty percent of children of 5 and 6 reply to the question by naming one or more wild animals, with snake, lion, tiger, and bear predominating. Sixty percent or more of children between the ages of 7 and 12 answer similarly but, after mental age 12, it is rare. ("What Children Fear," *Journal of Genetic Psychology* 106: 265–77, 1965)

The actual animals named ranged from the rare (crocodile, buffalo, eel, gorilla, whale, wolf) to the extinct (dinosaur), although some choices were sensible (bee, mosquito, scorpion, shark, tarantula, infected parakeet).

One five-year-old boy answered, "Dogs." When asked, "What else?" he answered, "Dog, dog, two dogs!"

"Anything else?"

"Ten dogs" was his final response, which, to the child, must have proved the adage Ask a stupid question and you get . . . what you deserve.

One valuable conclusion is Dr. Maurer's commentary on the effects of television. "Fright films would seem to be traumatic before the child thoroughly understands that they are only imaginary; after that age the possibility of their being therapeutic may enter. Age nine to 10 appears to be the dividing line."

One four-year-old we know came to his mother in tears because "they shot the white horse." It took considerable consoling before he began to comprehend that the horse, a highly trained and paid television actor, no doubt lived to ride again in another Western.

What to Do: Normal Fear of Animals

1. Identify for the child what is happening when you both meet a new animal. "Dogs can be scary, but let's see whether this one is friendly."

2. Teach proper guidelines for sensible treatment of, and conduct around, both pets and zoo animals.

3. Participation in the care and feeding of a pet helps a child better understand how animals both resemble and differ from humans.

4. Don't belittle a child's fear.

5. Barring a traumatic experience, such as getting bitten, most animal fears will remit by age seven.

6. Try not to transmit your own problems with animals or insects you may fear.

Fear of Animals: Traumatized Child

Janice, a bubbling four-year-old, was always playing. She would run, jump, and hide. One day she visited a neighbor who owned a very friendly German shepherd dog, King. Because Janice had outgrown her early, normal fear of dogs, she exuberantly pulled King's tail. Startled, the dog turned around, growled ferociously, and nipped the girl's hand.

Although Janice cried, she quieted after her mother held her and washed the bitten hand. Then the incident passed until three weeks later when Janice, seeing a dog being walked by its owner, refused to go out the front door of her house. Her fear increased until the girl became hysterical and clinging whenever she went anywhere near a dog. This behavior would not remit.

Motivation

Initially this kind of fear, based on injury or trauma from a specific and real animal, seems more sensible than the fanciful fears of monsters, witches, or dinosaurs. For that same reason, it also requires more treatment.

What to Do

1. Do not force the child into the dreaded situation or mock the child if he caused the incident through ignorance of animal ways.

2. If the fear persists or seems to increase, a phobia may be beginning. For further help, see Chapter 8 on nature-related phobias and the Afterword on what happens at a phobia center, or seek professional help.

FEAR OF NOISES
(AUDITORY FEARS: AGES FOUR THROUGH SIX)

About eight o'clock one night Peter and Johanna were watching television while four-year-old Marie played quietly with her dolls in her bedroom. Suddenly, however, a fire engine whizzed by outside the windows. Although Marie didn't see it, she ran into the living room, grabbed her mother's leg, and began crying furiously.

"What's the matter, darling?" her mother asked, but Marie couldn't talk. Her parents began to fear that something had happened in her room.

As the sound of the screaming engine faded into the distance, Marie's sobs relented, and she allowed her mother to lead her back to her room.

Definition

At four years of age various auditory fears surface. Fears of loud noises, such as fire engines or buzz saws, become increasingly difficult for the child to tolerate. Besides being startled, the child is genuinely disoriented until the noise passes, when he mysteriously quiets down.

Symptoms

1. Putting hands over ears while crying uncontrollably;
2. Running to the parent for comfort and protection;
3. Subsidence of the terror nearly as rapidly as it came on.

Motivation

In the time span of fears, about three-and-one-half years old can be an anxious age when a child seems to fear everything.

Furthermore, in some four-year-olds reemerges what greatly resembles the infant's startle reflex at loud or sudden noises, especially sirens, thunder, power mowers, dishwashers, or angry voices occurring at night. Indeed, what was a reflex posture of blinking eyes, bent neck, and open mouth in the infant has grown to an emotion, since the preschool child now exhibits more adult characteristics of fear, such as a rise in blood pressure and the release of stored glucose from the liver. (To read further on the biology of fear, proving that this emotion is physical as much as mental, see the Afterword.)

Although auditory fears lighten at five years, they may return at five-and-one-half through six with perhaps a new cast of villains—doorbells, flushing toilets, radio static, insect and bird noises.

The younger child's disorientation stems from the fact that he does not yet know the physical explanation or reasons for various pieces of loud machinery—their tasks or purposes.

What to Do

1. Reassure and comfort the child without belittling the seemingly excessive emotion.

2. Distract the child with a favorite activity or toy.

3. Teach the child to open his mouth or cover his ears to protect the eardrums during the passage of airplanes or fire engines.

4. Educate about the functions or habits of saws, ambulance sirens, morning crows, or whatever is terrifying the child. This will probably involve nothing more complicated than finding the item in a picture encyclopedia or getting a book from the library.

5. Remember that auditory fears are normal for this age group. The presence of such fears, although embarrassing in public, does not mean that your child will grow up strange or cowardly.

FEAR OF BED-WETTING (AGES THREE AND FOUR)

Ariane had just passed her third birthday. Bright and cheerful, she led her nursery class in activities. Since she had been successfully toilet trained at two-and-a-half, she woke every morning with a dry diaper. When she requested no more night diapers, her mother therefore trusted her to sleep and remain dry without one.

Shortly after this step into maturity Ariane became irritable, however. She fought going to sleep with a force reminiscent of her toddler year. Next she became more argumentative, refusing to perform simple tasks. When she begn awakening wet in the middle of the night, having soaked her bedding as well as herself, something was clearly wrong. After many questions, her mother finally revealed how much the little girl feared losing her newly won skill.

Symptoms

1. Irritability;
2. Night waking;
3. Regression to other earlier behaviors, such as baby talk, thumbsucking, or cloth chewing;
4. Anxiety.

Motivation

For the newly trained child, fear of bed-wetting is a subtle but real issue, since the training process introduces so many new issues and concerns.

Toilet training is a complex issue and involves the child's first awareness that he can control parental reaction. It is a way to please parents as one two-and-a-half-year-old said, "I think I'll go to the potty because it will make mommy very happy." Refusal to train is also a way to say no to parents' wishes.

Although the child desires to be as grown-up as possible, nighttime control depends on the maturity of the bladder muscles and so has little to do with conscious wishes, even in the child who has already progressed toward daytime dryness. On this issue, it is wise to avoid pushing him too quickly.

What to Do

1. Note any regression or change in behavior after your child begins sleeping without a diaper for nap or nighttime. Such change can indicate a reaction to the stress of the situation.

2. Take the child to the bathroom before bedtime and give few liquids after 6 P.M. The last person to bed at eleven or midnight can also walk the child to the bathroom.

3. Take care not to criticize or blame the child for "accidents," inconvenient as these are at 2 or 5 A.M.

4. If the child continues to show both difficult behavior and a return to wet diapers, use a nighttime diaper again. Explain that "big children" often wear night diapers so they can sleep well all through the night.

5. Do not feel that you or your child has "failed." With proper encouragement a normal child will train himself eventually. Be patient.

FEAR ABOUT GENITALS
(AGES THREE THROUGH FIVE)

Jennifer, a beautiful, petite three-year-old girl, came to her mother one morning. "Mommy," she said. "I've been bad." Only recently had she understood she could do "bad" things, like playing with her mother's china or turning on the phonograph.

Calmly her mother asked why Jennifer thought she was bad, expecting to hear about some violent swath of paint across one wall of her room.

"Because I don't have a pee-pee," answered Jennifer, straightfaced. "At school Jonathan showed me his pee-pee, and I don't have one so I must be bad. Somebody took it."

Definition

This fear involves frequent mention, worry, or guilt about the child's genitals, such as why boys and girls differ or what punishment the child may expect for having lost it (girls), shrunk it in the cold (boys), or just for owning it. On the last point, a friend of ours named Ann reported the following commentary, delivered by her three-year-old grandson as she bathed him one evening: "Look at my penis, Grandma. Isn't it beautiful? Are they going to cut it off?" The little fellow had recently heard circumcision discussed.

In toddlers just emerged from years of diapers and other padding, excessive attention to genitals in the form of masturbation is also common.

Symptoms

1. Younger children usually question why the visible differences between the sexes exist, since people's bodies, especially small children's, seem basically more similar (same number of arms, legs, ears, and so forth) than different.

2. Older children's questions show fear about the differences, orienting them to the same sex parent with whom they may be both competitive during work or play and then apologetic for wanting to compete.

Motivation

Whether you are psychoanalytically inclined or not, it is hard to deny either Sigmund Freud's influence or the Oedipal situation that exists in many families. At about four years of age, both boys and girls start desiring an exclusive relationship with the parent of the opposite sex—to the exclusion of the same-sex parent. Since this is the age when diapers no longer hinder masturbation, whether hidden or open, the boy, newly aware of his genitals, can easily worry that a jealous father will retaliate against his son's interest in the mother. Girls in love with their fathers also fear punishment.

Ultimately the normal child accepts the situation as it is (mother and father belong together), and the Oedipal stage passes by ages six to seven.

What to Do

1. Begin early with accurate sex education, guided by the child's age, questions, and vocabulary. If you do not like the popular sex education books, every encyclopedia and many dictionaries have simple, factual drawings of human anatomy. Such reference books also present the human reproductive system within the context of other body systems—circulatory, digestive, sensory, and so forth. This approach is very reassuring if you get tongue-tied or embarrassed. Do not overwhelm the child with information. Try to answer the questions about sex in a straightforward, understandable manner. Don't tell the child more than he asks for.

If embarrassment occurs, be aware of it, but try to continue anyway. Since some parents feel that sex education does not belong in school, then home becomes the only possible place for a child and an adult to discuss these matters sensibly.

2. Reassure your child about why sexual differences exist. The child will naturally assume that one set of equipment (probably the male) is "better than" the other. One good explanation is that both sets are required during adulthood to produce a baby and are beautiful.

3. Establish an appropriate relationship between each child and the opposite sex parent. Discourage, for example, sleeping together except during emergencies or illness. Many pediatricians also suggest that father and daughter—and mother and son—not bathe together after the child reaches two-and-a-half.

4. The working parent, perhaps a father, who travels frequently for long periods, may experience special problems relating again to a mother and son who have become a bonded couple during his absence. A mother who is ill may discover the same problem as her husband and daughter cooperate to perform many household tasks. Obviously it is impossible to schedule illness or the work demands of certain jobs, but be sensitive to the emotional dynamics of children aged four to seven.

FEAR OF ILLNESS IN A PARENT

Lindsay was three-and-one-half years old when her parents announced that they were going to take a special vacation on an airplane to go to California from New York. Everyone was excited about this prospect except her mother, Wendy, who the night before the flight registered a 100-degree fever. Thinking it was a flu that would abate in a day, everyone went on their way. Unfortunately, Wendy became quite ill, needing to stay bedridden for over one week.

Lindsay did not seem to have any adverse reaction until two weeks after her mother's recovery. At this time she became extremely fearful and clingy. She did not want to leave her mother to go to school and began having significant sleeping problems.

Definition

This is a normal fear, which develops when the child sees or hears of a situation that, based on people's reactions, appears dangerous or bad. There is often a one- to three-week delay before symptoms emerge.

Symptoms

1. Behavior typical of separation anxiety;
2. Difficulty sleeping, irritability, whining, clingy behavior.

Motivation

This fear obviously occurs when the child is afraid of something "bad" happening. The normal sense of well-being at home is disrupted, resulting in a fearful response from the child. This may emerge during any major life stress, such as an illness, a divorce, or a loss of job.

What to Do

1. Try to find a connection to the behavior that is difficult and the life stress. It may be difficult to put up with the child's actions when you are dealing with a hard situation. But understanding that the child is afraid of any change might help.

2. Try to calm the child and give him realistic, optimistic appraisal of the situation. "Mommy is sick, but the doctor was here to make her better. She'll be better soon. Remember when the doctor helped you the last time you were not feeling well?"

3. Allow the child to play out stories of the stressful situation. If a parent is ill, buy a toy doctor's or nurse's kit and encourage the child to make his dolls better.

4. If possible, keep the child's routine the same. Maintain the same bedtime, wake time, breakfast time, and so forth. Disruptive patterns that begin in response to a stress can often develop into habits if they are not corrected.

FEAR OF LOSING EMOTIONAL CONTROL
(FOUR AND FIVE YEARS OLD)

Now five, Peter had always been a handful. Nursery school teachers had phoned his parents on several occasions because of his scuffling with other children. Part of the problem stemmed from his parents' disagreement about the best way to discipline him. Although his mother sought strictness, his father often relented, at first passively behind her back, then openly by saying "Well, your mother won't like this, but you're only young once" when he allowed Peter to stay up late, eat between meals, or try out the dangerous skateboard that his mother was "keeping" for him until he got bigger. This created a pattern at home that both allowed the child his way too often and left him confused about when and whether he would be disciplined for disobeying his mother's rules.

One night, however, his father was working late when his mother wanted to get him ready for bed. "It's time to brush teeth, honey," she said.

"Just five more minutes," he replied. "I'm watching TV."

Angered, his mother yelled, "Turn that thing off and get upstairs *now*."

While his mother fumed, Peter shouted, "No, no, no!"

"If you don't get upstairs right now, you won't watch TV for a week, and I mean it."

Slowly Peter rose. Next he kicked the end table beside the couch, crashing a lamp to the floor. After an instant of fear flashed across his face, he retreated to his room. His mother stood speechless.

During the following hours, he awoke twice with nightmares, and the next day his behavior ricocheted between extremes of docility and irritability.

Symptoms

> **1.** Irritability following an emotional outburst;
> **2.** Sleep disturbance;
> **3.** Distractibility.

Motivation

Youngsters of this age often fear some of their emotions, particularly when bad consequences result from their actions. Everything is, of course, aggravated when parents lack consistency in setting limits for acceptable behavior. The paradox with this situation is that the more "lenient" parents are, the more confused a child is about what's allowed or not.

What to Do

1. Help the child maintain control of himself by setting firm limits.

2. If parents do not agree on standards for behavior, see the What to Do section of Fears About Inconsistent Discipline (Chapter 2).

3. If the child refuses to do what you ask, continue to firmly insist. Design a clear system of consequences and rewards for the child, and use it.

4. If the child threatens to lose control, become violent or destructive, tell him that you do not permit this—that the same consequences and rewards operate here also.

FEAR OF BAD THOUGHTS: OEDIPAL ISSUES
(FIVE AND SIX YEARS OLD)

Five-year-old Billy was struggling with the classic situation of wanting his mother all to himself. He elaborated for her the ways in which the two of them would go off, get married, find a pretty house, and live happily ever after. "Mommy, I'm gonna marry you," he declared. "We'll be so happy."

As he wove his tales, his amused mother would say that because she was married already, she couldn't marry Billy although she loved him madly. "You know I can't love a little boy more than I already love you, Billy," she insisted.

One day when his father arrived home exhausted from work, Billy confronted him. "I hate you, Daddy. I wish you never existed!"

The startled father stared at Billy, laughed, and then walked in to see his wife.

Because Billy's own outburst frightened him, he became extremely clingy with his mother that evening and the next day.

Symptoms

1. Regressive behavior;
2. Clingy, frightened behavior after an outburst.

Motivation

At this age, the child is filled with powerful emotions that he does not know how to direct. Billy's Oedipal problem happens with all children. As the son feels upset with his father, he also fears some terrible punishment, since angry fathers can do appalling things.

As the child discovers that his emotions are either safe or not taken seriously by their intended "victim," he becomes less frightened.

What to Do

1. If you see the child frightened after some outburst, try to understand the situation and forgive it. This may be diffi-

cult, because the very behavior that is symptomatic of the fear that afflicts the child may have exhausted your patience and sympathy or at least annoyed you.

2. Set firm, consistent limits so that the child cannot act in a manner later to be feared by himself. For example, if the child insults or attacks a parent, say, "You may not speak like that (do that) to your father (or mother). If you do it again, you will be sent to your room." Then keep your resolve to discipline the child for the kind of behavior that frightens everyone.

FEAR OF THE CRIPPLED OR HANDICAPPED

John was four-and-one-half years old when he saw the crippled man. The boy was playing in the park with his mother and some friends when the man hobbled past on crutches. John took one look and ran away. For the next three weeks John asked his mother so many questions about being crippled that she couldn't concentrate on his brother and sister and finally yelled at him to stop.

Definition

This fear is shown by repeated and overwhelming concern. from the child that he will also become, for example, crippled or blind, lose a leg and need a wheelchair, or become otherwise handicapped.

Symptom

Persistent fixation or questioning upon or after the sight of someone whose body is maimed or different.

Motivation

Fear of the crippled or maimed occurs in preschool children, already feeling vulnerable, who worry that the condition may be contagious. "Can this happen to me (or someone close to me)?" is the essence of the disturbance. The fear is that of contagion.

What to Do

1. As with sex education, alleviating this fear requires some anatomical or medical knowledge. Try to explain the particular illness or accident that the person endured. Although researchers are still puzzling out exact mechanisms behind afflictions like Alzheimer's disease or multiple sclerosis, explaining how someone loses an arm or leg in a machine or auto accident—or the use of the same limbs after a cerebral hemorrhage—is tragically simple. Obviously, one wants to reassure the child and not frighten him.

2. Use words like, "It's scary to see somebody so different, but the world has many kinds of people. That person was sick (or in a bad accident), but that *disease* or *problem isn't catching.* It's not like a cold or chicken pox."

3. Be tolerant of the child's questions.

4. Stress the need for the same good manners (consideration) toward the handicapped that he should show to anyone.

FEAR OF INJURY, ESPECIALLY FALLING (AGE FIVE)

Five-year-old Lindsay was having a great day. She and her parents had just visited the top of the Empire State Building and were about to walk down a short flight of stairs to the elevator.

As she began descending, however, Lindsay froze. Fear

flashed from her eyes, and panic came across her face. "No. I can't," she cried. "I won't go down—no, no!"

Speaking gently, her mother bent over her. "Come on, dear. Let's go down so we can have lunch."

But Lindsay's legs would not move. The scene persisted until the girl had attracted the attention of every tourist around the observation deck.

Definition and Symptoms

Fear and sometimes panic at the possibility of physical hurt from everyday activities.

Motivation

A combination of awkwardness and inattention to details of physical location (failure to notice objects on floor, number of stairs, uneven sidewalks, and so forth), causes some children to trip easily and hurt themselves at this age. Unlike the toddler, the five-year-old now possesses the agility to perform actions like climbing trees or boulders yet lacks the seven-year-old's discrimination—the ability to extricate himself, to know he shouldn't have attempted it in the first place.

This realistic fear of harmful activities contrasts with the six-year-old's exaggerated drama over small bruises or scratches (see Chapter 4).

There is a new trend in physical education for kindergarten through third grade, away from pushing the child into competition or even free-form games. It involves rather the teaching of basic movements as a life skill rather than competition—how to run without falling, how to move safely across a field or gym with twenty other children also in motion, how to follow verbal directions, how to watch and imitate an activity. All such practice teaches cooperation, good judgment, and proper timing—minus the tension of "winning" or "losing."

What to Do

1. Help the child assess the reality of situations in which he could actually get hurt and those that are safe.

2. If the child gets into a difficult position, avoid the words "You got yourself up (or in) there. Now get yourself out," especially if, as with Lindsay, the child did not plan or willfully enter the predicament.

3. To avoid future episodes, say something like, "That was pretty scary, huh? How do you think we can keep it from happening again?" Remember that the goal here is to help the child feel secure (neither abandoned nor smarting from recrimination) and yet to teach a lesson.

FEAR OF GETTING LOST
(AGE FIVE-AND-ONE-HALF)

Bobby had generally been a most secure little fellow. He'd adjusted to nursery school and always done well socially. One day he and his parents were shopping at a crowded local mall. After a fine lunch they were looking at clothing in a store when Bobby grabbed his father's hand and started screaming.

"Don't go, Daddy. I don't want to leave here."

His mother now rushed to him and asked what had happened.

At first he couldn't answer, just looked down and shuffled his feet. "You'll go. You'll go!" he finally sobbed as he stared and pointed out through the store's open doorway.

When his parents couldn't get him to leave the store with them, his mother discovered "nothing" had happened—except a mélange of insecurity, confusion, and terror of the vast open space outside that suddenly clutched Bobby. Right beyond the shop's entrance began the multilevels of noise, music, crying babies, and milling crowds that seemed to extend forever.

Definition

Fear of getting lost in woods, crowds, or stores is the form that *spatial fear* typically takes at this age. It heaps visual flooding upon the meager resources, especially of the tired or insecure child.

Symptoms

1. Abrupt expression of panic, punctuated by fitful insecurity about getting lost or finding oneself alone;
2. Anxiety and crying, particularly in situations of "blooming, buzzing confusion" (such as crowds, parades, and fairs).

Motivation

Both the sudden onset and extreme reactions produced by this fear can be unnerving to the parent, who reasonably concludes that "nothing" has happened. What has happened is the child's realization of his continuing vulnerability combined with inability to be alone. A younger child, left alone, will probably play for a while before panicking, while an older one can better assess whom to ask or what to do to obtain help without hysteria.

What to Do

1. If your child is at this age or stage, prepare him with coping strategies before or as you enter the situation. "We're going shopping here and here" (point at the stores or street corners). "We'll all stay close together, but if we get separated, meet at the front door of (store name) or at (some store counter or landmark)." Emphasize, "We would never leave without you."

2. Also show him the floor level or number you're on, since all floors of a mall or department store tend to look alike.

3. Instruct the child about asking a store employee, not a stranger, how to find the entrance or a certain counter within the store.

4. Reassure the child by these sensible measures without dramatizing the possibility of getting lost.

FEAR ABOUT DAY CARE OR KINDERGARTEN

Four-year-old Chad eagerly awaited going to "school," since his mother and father had been so enthusiastic about this landmark day in his life. When the morning arrived, everyone was very excited. While his mother walked him to school, he felt proud and happy.

As she left, however, the situation changed. Chad *wanted* her and didn't know where she went or why she had to leave. Although a teacher was trying to be nice to him, she only frightened him. The other children were playing by themselves, yet he had no desire to join them. Noticing the room's dark corners made his stomach sink.

He didn't want to be here; "school" was all a mistake. Now he knew he didn't ever want to be away from Mommy again.

Definition

This fear of going to school, especially on the first day or after the child has been home ill, is marked by significant resistance in the form of complaints and ultimately tantrums.

Symptoms

    1. Verbal complaints, such as "That school is yucky" or "The teacher is gross";

2. Crying;
3. Clinging;
4. In the extreme case, vomiting and symptomatic illness.

Motivation

This fear can occur abruptly during the period from three through five years old. Some anxiety is normal, of course, as the child anticipates the opening days of school or of any novel situation away from home for the first time. It may also occur while and until the child gets his bearings and becomes familiar with the class and teacher.

The parent should differentiate between fear of leaving home (entering the new situation) and fear of something traumatic that may have occurred at school. If nothing untoward has occurred in school, then what the child fears is leaving home—separation anxiety.

This form of separation anxiety may relate directly to a parent's own ambivalence about the child's leaving home for the first time, which may be expressed as fretting over the weather, the child's health, or the doubtful quality of future playmates. Parents often want children to go off and be with others and attend day care, but sometimes it is normal to be hesitant to let the child go. The reasons for this can range from the parent not wanting to be alone to being overly protective. The perceptive child responds by choosing not to attend school.

What to Do

1. Try to learn what is going on at school that is upsetting the child. If you discover nothing significant, firmly and caringly instruct the child that he must attend school. Clarify

when and where you or the school bus will pick up the child after school, and be prompt about your part of this.

2. If the above fails, escort the child to school and speak with school personnel about their preferred way to handle the situation. Often a child will be fine as soon as a parent walks out the door. It eases some situations, however, if the parent remains for a part of the school day. The school should be able to advise you.

3. Examine your own motives for any hidden messages you may be giving the child.

4. If the problem occurs on the first day of school, assume the reaction expresses a fear of separating from you. Follow steps 2 and 3.

5. If the fear does not relate to parental ambivalence, help familiarize the child with the school and his class. Reassure and support the child by discussing something that was enjoyable about the school experience, perhaps new friends and toys or lunch.

FEAR OF LOSS OF PARENT (AGES FOUR AND FIVE)

Four-year-old Linda was always a happy child. One day while she played at a good friend's house, her mother left her there in order to run some errands.

Suddenly Linda stopped playing and looked up. "Where's Mommy?" she asked. She was told that her mother had driven away but would return shortly. Forlorn, Linda began to wail and couldn't be comforted despite everyone's best efforts.

For the moment Linda truly believed that her mother was not coming back for her. Although the thought had nothing to do with reality, she nevertheless believed her mother wouldn't return.

Definition

This fear of loss of parent, particularly mother, is so prominent—however irrational—in the minds of four- and five-year-olds that it must be considered normal.

Symptoms

1. Prevailing panic upon realization that the parent has left;
2. Disconsolate refusal to listen to logic about the problem;
3. Prevalence of the fear over all other emotions;
4. Abrupt cessation of symptoms upon parent's return.

Motivation

This fear recapitulates earlier childhood experience of separation anxiety, when the child feared loss or deprivation of the nurturing parent, no matter whether the parent or the child has only temporarily left the scene. That is, the fear that the mother won't return or won't be there when the child returns are but twin forms of the same emotion. Moreover, although Linda mourned the absence of her mother, the father or other caretaker can as easily become the focus of the fear.

Another common reason for panic with this fear occurs in the child who is angry at the parent, whom he then wishes far away or even dead. Suddenly the wish seems to have come true, overwhelming the child's psyche.

What to Do

1. Advise the child of your imminent departure and be specific about when you will return. Be extremely prompt.

2. If your child has just begun suffering anxiety attacks, do the following immediately: State that you are leaving but will return in five minutes. Be prompt.

When the child tolerates this, extend your time out of the home to fifteen minutes, next to one-half hour. Be as consistent as you can.

Gradually extend the time to what you require.

3. When you return, reward the child with hugs and praise for having tolerated your absence.

4. Do not try a new baby-sitter during this period.

5. If the problem does not remit despite reassurance and consistency, consult professional help.

FEAR ABOUT DEATH

In the book *Who Is Sylvia?,* writer Lucy Freeman describes a vulnerable five-year-old's first realization of the power of death. Ironically it occurred during an outing meant to entertain her.

One afternoon that winter my father bundled me into coat, hat and mittens. He took me to the aquarium at Battery Park on the southern tip of Manhattan. I walked in awe past tank after tank of brilliantly colored fish from far countries. My father read me their esoteric names engraved on the tanks.

Suddenly my eyes were drawn to the ceiling. A titanic dead turtle, twice the size of a man, dangled in the air, suspended a foot from the top. This was the first time death held reality—if the turtle could die, so could I. The blackness of the turtle, the bigness of it, the unearthly stillness of it. . . . I was afraid it would fall on me, crush me, join me to it in oblivion. I tugged at my father's coat, pleaded, even while I stared mesmerized at the dark turtle floating in the air. "Let's get out of here."

"It's dead. It can't hurt you."

This account is paradoxical because what reassures the adult —namely, the stillness of death—is exactly what frightens the child, who does not yet differentiate between herself and a now inanimate object.

Definition

Curiosity about death, as about birth, is normal for the developing child. What is abnormal is extreme concern about the topic in a healthy child who suddenly begins to worry that he or someone he loves will drop dead or die soon.

Symptoms

1. Refusal to look at dead animals or other creatures;
2. The opposite reaction: preoccupation with, or talking about, death.

Motivation

A child's understanding of death has several stages. For the young child, it means mainly separation from a loved one. Until age five, it is seen as a departure, a further existence under other conditions. Since for these children death has no finality, the five-year-old John Kennedy, Jr., could stand beside the assassinated President Kennedy's coffin waving a flag that he planned "to take home to Daddy." Sometimes, however, the youngster angrily blames the dead person or other relatives for causing the death.

From ages five to ten, death can be personified as a being who carries others off; this is a prelude to the adolescent and adult understanding of disease or accident as factors.

As Lucy Freeman indicates above, the average child does not fear death at all until he has seen its power acting upon some person or animal. And it is only when the child has understood that the dead person isn't just sleeping and won't come back that questions such as "Can I die, too?" or "Will I catch it?" arise. In that moment the child feels his own vulnerability.

To summarize the differing reactions, compare this story involving the three-year-old's resentment at his father's death (and how it affected his adult life) with five-year-old Lucy above. The writer is Max Cleland, who grew up to become secretary of state for Georgia.

> Though I couldn't really remember him as I grew up, there was that indefinable sense of rejection within me . . . a child somehow feels abandoned by the mother or father who dies.
>
> Mother loved and cared for me. But without realizing it at the time I know now that I suffered from not having a father's love. Subconsciously, I suppose, I also resented him for leaving us. As I grew older, I believe that this resentment was transferred to almost every man with whom I came in contact.
>
> He was an adversary to overcome. He was a competitor in business, a challenger on the tennis courts, and in every instance, someone with whom to match wits. Even in middle age I did not realize I was still crippled in a man-to-man relationship. (*Plus, The Magazine of Positive Thinking* 37:6, July/August 1986)

What to Do

1. Remember that awareness and fear of death are a normal part of being in the world. Educate the child about death, but tell him that he need not worry about it. The child's preoccupations will usually pass.

Reassure the child that, in ordinary circumstances, he need not fear death for himself. Say something like, "Yes, it happened to Grandpa. But it's nothing you should worry about right now." In the more threatening case of a parent's death, stress that it's quite unusual for someone of Daddy's or Mommy's age to die; that people are normally quite old when they die.

2. If someone close to the child dies, answer resulting questions honestly according to your own religious or other beliefs. Remember that mere "old age" is usually not a sufficient reason to die. To a child, anyone over twenty, including you, is "old"!

If the death occurred not from disease but from an accident that might have been prevented, discuss this with the child if you can, with commonsense discussions about using seatbelts and obeying speed limits if it was an auto fatality, plus whatever other safety procedures help show that even accidental deaths do not happen for no reason at all.

3. Learn the child's feelings as you speak about the loved one.

4. If you are heavily involved yourself in care for a dying relative, try to remember that a child also may be feeling lonely, confused, or upset by the drastic changes in family mood or schedule, and this may increase his worry about death. In the presence of death, we are all afraid, but the child needs to understand that he did not cause the death nor need he worry about its happening to him tomorrow.

5. The following recommendations apply regarding the presence of children over five years of age at the funeral home. If you are able to discuss grieving with the child and the youngster's questions seem motivated by curiosity rather than terror, it is appropriate to take a child or children to the funeral home for a few minutes. Phrase it simply in terms of "saying good-bye" or whatever seems natural to you, and be guided by the child's reactions at the home or to the coffin. It is not recommended that young children attend the burial itself.

CHAPTER 4

. . .

The Scary World:
Fears of Six- Through
Ten-Year-Olds

TYPICAL FEARS OF SIX-YEAR-OLDS

During the year a child becomes six, her fears will probably both intensify and specialize. A fear of dogs now centers on "big dogs"; a spatial fear localizes to the attic, cellar, or other particular place in house or neighborhood.

Other typical fears of this age involve monsters, wild animals, insects, sounds (storm, wind, toilet flushing, motors), injury, water or getting her face wet (especially during shampoos), deformed people, lateness to school, and worry that parent may die.

TYPICAL FEARS OF SEVEN-YEAR-OLDS

At this age many previous fears can resolve, primarily because the child is apt to be both more cautious and better able to handle difficult situations by negotiation and sensible protection (asking an adult to precede the child into a dark room, practicing putting her face under water when swimming).

Nevertheless, normal fears involve ghosts and shadows (visual), heights (spatial), spies and burglars, adoption, being late to school, entering new situations, and social rejection.

FEAR OF MONSTERS (SIX- AND SEVEN-YEAR-OLDS)

Robby, six years old, lived alone with his mother. The two of them had successfully endured an early childhood illness, which had been extremely trying. At five, Bobby had started talking and worrying about a monster that now lived in the ceiling of his room, having slithered down the airshaft from outdoors. Although the monster had no name and Robby couldn't describe it exactly, he was sure it lurked there above his bed as soon as darkness came. He remained nervous about this new visitor until his mother suggested that together they say good night to it during every bedtime.

The poor creature, who couldn't stand such friendliness, disappeared after two months.

Motivation

This fear of imaginary creatures of various kinds can increase through age seven. Although it may be inspired by television or the child's reading, it usually stems from the youngster's own development. By the age of six, a child is clearly aware of reality, but imagination still figures vividly in helping to resolve conflicts. That is, children often attribute human traits, both good and bad, to imaginary creatures to which they may assign vivid roles for good or evil. Through her imaginary friends, the relatively helpless child can project the power and allies she needs to help her cope with the large, frightening world.

A friendly genie, for instance, can magically find a lost wallet —or even regain Daddy's lost job. On the dark side, a monster with big teeth can kill the meanest teacher or neighborhood bully, and the child will be neither suspected nor blamed. When you realize that the average cartoon program is filled with horrific creatures doing violence to each other and the landscape, you see that the child need look no further than Saturday morning TV to meet monsters of appropriate power and violence.

Symptoms

1. Child's direct statement that she fears a monster that resides in some particular place;
2. Refusal to enter this place;
3. Failure of parental logic ("Of course, there's no ghost. I was just up there") to modify the situation.

What to Do

1. See suggestions for reality orienting and monster proofing in first two sections (Fear of the Dark and Bedtime, Fear of Monsters, Ghosts, Witches, and Other Creatures) of Chapter 3. By age seven or eight, the child has begun to control the environment (and the fear) by making sensible requests, such as for a flashlight or for an adult to precede her into a dark closet or attic.

2. Know that a child of this age localizes the monster threat to a specific place in the neighborhood or house, such as the cellar or attic. Monsters no longer float freely, attacking anywhere.

3. Don't belittle the child, even when you believe she is acting "like a baby."

4. Help the child test reality by looking around the cellar, attic, or cave with you once, but do not let yourself be forced into this every afternoon or night.

5. Reassure the child that she is safe from these scary things, that you'll tuck in the sheets extra-tight, leave a light burning, stay in the house—promise whatever you can honestly commit to.

6. Reward the child each time she can "overpower" the monster alone, using the techniques just listed. Verbal praise is effective.

FEAR OF SPACES

Caroline, seven-and-a-half years old, was always regarded by her mother as a mature, sophisticated young lady. Near bedtime one night, however, having run to her mother in the kitchen, Caroline said, "Mommy, I don't want to go to sleep."

"But you must," answered the mother, "or you'll be tired at school tomorrow."

"No! I heard a sound in the attic, and I'm not going to sleep," the girl declared.

After an hour's discussion, argument, and convincing beyond any reasonable doubt that the attic was uninhabited, Caroline finally went to her room—accompanied by her mother, who was also required to sit with her at bedtime for the next three weeks.

Ultimately Caroline developed a complex ritual by which to avoid looking at the attic door whenever she entered or left her room. This behavior would not remit for a year, until she was eight-and-a-half.

Definition

This is a fear of what may lurk in particular places about the home or neighborhood, such as closets, attics, cellars, haunted houses, caves, and hollow trees. A child who no longer fears sleeping alone or worries about the visible dark may fret now about what she *cannot* see.

Symptoms

1. Refusal to go alone to certain parts of the house, especially at night;
2. Imagining familiar objects or places fraught with sinister possibility, including ghosts, monsters, or terrors from TV.

Motivation

Again the visitation of hostile or fearsome monsters upon familiar settings shows the child's active imagination, besides providing an outlet for aggressive or other unpleasant feelings. Localizing the danger to a single place helps the child compartmentalize and contain it.

What to Do

Follow procedures listed in the previous section.

FEAR OF ANIMALS (AGES SIX THROUGH TEN)

Symptoms

1. Fearful expression when confronted with an animal;
2. Crying or clinging;
3. Avoidance of a situation that involves facing an animal.

Motivation

Fear of animals is usual for children in this age range, although its form and focus change as the child matures. Furthermore, the child's reaction will vary according to personal experience. The child who has a dog, for instance, and considers it a friend will probably react with less fear to a strange dog.

During these years the average child fears a more realistic selection of animals—large dogs instead of all dogs, lizards or frogs instead of dinosaurs.

What to Do

See suggestions in Chapter 3 for normal fears of animals and those based upon traumatic experience, such as a dog bite.

FEAR OF BEING LATE TO SCHOOL
(SIX YEARS OLD)

Johnny's parents were ecstatic about his entrance into first grade in a good school. When he received glowing reports from his teacher after the first week, they couldn't have been happier. From babyhood Johnny had been a bubbly child who slept and ate well.

One morning during the second week of school, however,

he changed, jumping out of bed at 6 A.M. instead of his usual 7:15. His mother found him, nervous and excited, pacing the living room and hall. "What time is it?" he demanded.

Aware of his recent fascination with telling time, she still had to spend twenty minutes questioning him before he admitted, "I'm really scared I'll be late to school."

On the one hand, his concern was praiseworthy; on the other, he was clearly agitated.

Finally she discovered that he had been reprimanded by the principal in front of classmates when he arrived late one morning of the previous week. His shame had developed into a preoccupation.

Definition

This fear usually develops from the trauma attendant upon a previous incident of lateness.

Symptoms

1. Agitation and excitability;
2. Compulsive looking at watches and clocks.

Motivation

Since school rapidly becomes the focus of a normal child's social life, experiencing a situation that can be construed as traumatic can cause a child to fear a repetition.

Unlike many fears discussed in this book, this fear is highly situational—not developmental in the strict sense of that word, although an afflicted child must be old enough to understand the operation of cause and effect. The fear is a reaction to the consequences of being late.

What to Do

1. Find out what occurred at school to make your child anxious.

2. Speak with the school authorities to prevent a recurrence.

3. Increase the child's understanding of time so she will not wrongly estimate how much time is actually available before some event.

4. Show the child how to set and use an alarm clock. Besides getting her up, it teaches the value of future planning.

5. Encourage the child in a regular schedule, especially about bedtime and awakening. This will provide reassurance.

6. If the child compulsively times the trip to school by watch or clock, provide a toy or book on the way as a distraction to allay anxiety.

SEPARATION ANXIETY, INCLUDING FEAR OF PARENT DYING

Richard was a bright, almost brilliant, seven-year-old who functioned well, patterning himself after his parents, who were both successful, interesting, and exciting people.

One afternoon he was scheduled to visit a friend's house for swimming. Since it was a hot summer, his mother was surprised when he refused to go. Because she had made plans to see a movie with a friend, her son's reluctance created some tension. After Richard, strong-willed as usual, again refused to leave and fell into a tantrum, his mother offered to stay with him at his friend's house.

Moreover, Richard's fears of leaving home intensified until questioning finally uncovered their source—the family's move from one house to another about six months earlier. Around the moving time his overworked parents often argued. When the arguing made him anxious, Richard had developed a fear of leaving his mother, although its symptoms did not emerge until several months after the incidents that prompted it.

Definition

As with younger children, this fear manifests itself by refusal to leave the parent to attend school or other activities.

Symptoms

1. A wide array, from mild disagreement to active protest when leaving the parent;
2. Physical symptoms of anxiety, such as crying, perspiration, headache, stomachache, vomiting, or diarrhea;
3. Possible delayed reaction of two weeks to one month.

Motivation

Fear of leaving home is again an example of separation anxiety. Such anxiety most often occurs for any of three reasons: (1) the parent—perhaps unconsciously—doesn't want the child to leave; (2) the leaving child fears something (death, illness) will happen to an at-home parent during her absence; (3) the at-home child fears losing a parent who is leaving the house, if only for work.

In the first situation, the parent's role is difficult to discern and admit. That is, the parent may think that he is delighted to have the child leave the house, indeed considering as nonsense the idea that a six- or eight-year-old should spend every free minute at home. All of us, however, may need the kind of companionship or attention that a child can lavish, and although it makes no lasting sense for either party, the parent doesn't want the child to leave. Since most children possess sonarlike intuition, a child can quickly sense this desire and respond.

In the second situation, the child fears that some disaster will occur if she does not remain with the loved, if sometimes difficult, parent. Sample misfortunes can range from fears about getting lost, parents dying, arguing, or losing jobs to the house burning down.

Often such fears relate to the child's own hostile feelings. Suppose, for instance, that the child is angry at the mother for temporarily forbidding TV until homework is done or a bedroom cleaned up. Uncomfortable with the anger, the child projects it via a fantasy in which the house catches fire. The child later feels she must stay at home to interrupt this "event."

Although each of these situations differs in its complex sequence of events, all result in the same symptom—the homebody child.

What to Do

1. Assess the problem carefully. See whether there is an actual reason that a previously sociable child refuses to go out, such as a fight or other incident that occurred at a friend's house.

2. Try to understand what the child feels. Although empathy matters, don't overdisplay emotion or attention to the complaint, or it may worsen—the child may see your concern as a way of getting extra attention.

3. If no untoward incident has occurred on the outside, encourage the child to leave as directly as possible. If you meet refusal, offer to remain with her at the friend's house, for instance, during part of the time. Each time your presence is required, stay a shorter period until the child can remain alone.

4. If you discover that *you* do not want the child to leave, remember that this is normal for many parents, especially with the child who acts young, fragile, or timid. Being sufficiently

brave to analyze your own reaction to your child's maturing, if only to leave your house for the next street, is the first step to changing that reaction.

FEAR OF NEW SITUATIONS: NEIGHBORHOOD, SCHOOL, CLUB, FRIENDS (SEVEN-YEAR-OLD)

When the five Smiths, parents and children, moved to their new home, all seemed happy. The house, located in a better section of town, was nevertheless a bargain; even the school was better. Although Gerry, who was seven at this time, liked the yard, which was large, he hated the house. He would not visit his room (away on the third floor) without accompaniment and, once there, insisted immediately upon leaving it. Next he complained that he couldn't sleep without his mother nearby, and he began refusing to attend school.

Symptoms

1. Reluctance, anxiety, or dread about the anticipated move or group;
2. Obsessive questioning about related details;
3. Refusal to enter the new situation alone.

Motivation

Fear of new situations is more difficult at this age than others, since a move seems to matter more or most to a child who has carefully built a routine on which he depends for security. Unfamiliar situations thus directly threaten the fragile sense of control that the cautious seven-year-old has managed to achieve in her young life.

What to Do

1. Prepare the child by describing or otherwise anticipating the new move or activity with photos or picture books. If the child becomes anxious, recall the last time she felt this way and managed to survive it.

2. Answer questions carefully.

3. Try to reassure the child with information and without paying undue attention to the anxiety.

4. If possible before the move, explore the new house and neighborhood together several times to acquaint the child with the area and possible playmates.

5. After the move, tour the house with the child to orient her. Draw diagrams or maps, if necessary, to show where family members will sleep and to indicate the school, your place of work, shopping center, and other landmarks.

FEAR OF ADOPTION (SEVEN-YEAR-OLD)

Stephanie, blond, athletic, and energetic, was just seven years old. She had a baby brother five years her junior and two parents who loved each other. It was a happy situation.

Therefore, when she returned from school one day asking whether she was adopted, her parents laughed. "Adopted?" they asked. "Why, we wanted you so much and were lucky to have you. You weren't adopted," they insisted, "but it might have been easier for your mother in the ninth month if you were." Both laughed.

Stephanie, however, did not relent. For several weeks she demanded reassurance until her questions became bothersome, mystifying her parents. She was quite annoying.

Finally they discovered that one of Stephanie's friends, whom she much admired, had discussed her own adoption. Thus Stephanie began fearing she, too, had been adopted.

Definition

In this "fantasy fear," a child imagines that he is not truly the daughter or son of the parents.

Symptoms

1. Preoccupation to the point of obsession with the topic of adoption;
2. Incessant questioning about it.

Motivation

At seven the child, who still thinks literally or, to put it in academic language, concretely, commonly wonders about an issue like adoption. Although she can control or handle many aspects of the household or neighborhood, an absolute assurance about something that can't even be remembered—the facts surrounding her birthday—is harder to achieve. For many children, the fear of not having one's real parents (or the successful search for better ones) becomes a fantasy game.

What to Do

1. For imagined adoption, simply reassure the child, "You *are* our little girl (or boy)." If the child knows something of the birth process, say, "Remember when we talked about having babies? Your mother and I had you that way, and we love you very much."

2. Recall the principle about neither under- nor overestimating the fear. Neither belittle nor overreact.

3. If your child was in fact adopted, it is often helpful to have told her, in very positive terms, about this reality before the age of seven.

SCHOOL AVOIDANCE (AGES SIX THROUGH TEN)

Motivation

School avoidance motivated by separation anxiety or parental suggestion can reappear at ages six (the beginning of first grade) and ten.

What to Do

1. See suggestions in Fear About Day Care or Kindergarten, Chapter 3.
2. For school avoidance based on fear of peer interaction, see the next section.
3. For avoidance based on other fears of school events involving popularity, performance, competition, public speaking, drugs, see Chapter 5.
4. For a fuller description of school avoidance, consult Chapter 7.

TYPICAL FEARS OF EIGHT-YEAR-OLDS

Instead of frankly expressing dread, eight-year-olds can be great worriers, compulsively repeating a situation, such as walking along a certain street, to exorcise or master a fear. They may also worry about being criticized, not liked, failing, and being punished. Girls are apt to fear meeting strange men, both real and imaginary. Eight-year-olds can also delight in teasing younger children by scaring them.

At the age of eight, a child is apt deliberately to repeat a fearful situation as a means to resolve it. This is the beginning of semiscientific experimentation. For example, the child may choose the route to school that passes the German shepherd, instead of going to all lengths to avoid the dog.

FEAR OF SOCIAL REJECTION (PEER INTERACTION)

Patrick was eight years old. His parents lived in a suburban community where one day Patrick hurried home from school in tears. His mother couldn't figure out what had happened.

Just before bedtime, however, Patrick revealed that he wouldn't ever visit his friend Jimmy's house again. In fact, he was never going to school again.

Apparently Jimmy had called him "a chicken" for not insulting a group of girls, and Patrick was not only hurt but frightened that rumors of his cowardice would spread until he found himself excluded from his group of friends. His fear was so real that he needed several hours after the incident before he could discuss exactly what had happened.

Definition

This fear stems from the child's growing awareness of, and preoccupation with, her peer group's reactions to her and each other.

Symptoms

1. Fear that the child won't be liked;
2. Worry over proper clothing, shoes, expressions, lunches, and so forth;
3. Conformity to any or all of these "standards," regardless of adult reactions;
4. Reports of social interactions, games, or events whenever the child feels left out.

Motivation

The age of seven marks the shift in a child's focus away from home exclusively and into the larger world of a peer group and the continuing socialization process of school. From seven through eleven years of age, the child thus intensifies her attachment to same-sex role models and friends outside the family. These years are also the time for bursts of organized sports and game-playing, based on structured rules and considerable cooperation.

All these factors create social hierarchies that dictate a child's position, although friendships are more fluid than they will be during the teen years. Thus, the child who painfully laments exclusion from a party or club may soon become a part of the same social group that previously rejected her. During these years, the club may also develop into a clique whose members may bully other children or rival another clique.

Often the child will refuse to discuss rejection with a parent, lest she appear "chicken" or "babyish," since it is humiliating to admit that youngsters known for years are suddenly ignoring or tormenting her.

Fears of rejection can be painful but ultimately useful to the child's learning to be independent and self-sustaining.

What to Do

1. Empathize with your child. Imagine yourself in her situation and see what you would feel. Share this with the child. Say, for example, "Oh, that must feel awful. I would feel upset about that."

2. Take care, however, to respect the fine line between empathy and overattention, which results in reinforcing the child's behavior.

3. Next, help the child learn some constructive skills to change the situation by changing either personnel or attitude. "Let's look at who your good friends are—who you can play with this week. And sometimes people change friends. Somebody who's giving you a hard time may change his mind next week."

4. Use this opportunity to teach how to choose friends—people who are fun to be with but also honest and dependable, not bullying or domineering.

5. Teach defenses against feeling badly, including the ancient adage "Sticks and stones will break my bones, but names will never hurt me."

FEAR OF CRITICISM (AGE EIGHT)

Eight-year-old Adam was always a good student, but this year his teachers noted that doing any work at school made him "nervous." On several occasions when in art class he would begin a drawing but, halfway through, would rip it up. Then he'd start again, this time quite behind the other children, who were nearly finished.

After he'd completed part of one picture, he crumpled it, then broke into sobs. When the teacher came to see what troubled him, he said, "It's awful, terrible. I hate it. I'm just no good." He finally cried so much that the teacher had to take him to the nurse's office.

Definition

At school, the child who fears criticism is hypercritical of her own work. At home she acts fearful and avoids direct interaction with parents during household jobs or homework sessions.

Symptoms

1. Avoidance of situations with potential for criticism, especially by parents;

2. Lying, denying, secretiveness about schoolwork;
3. Anxiety over performance.

Motivation

These fears crop up when the child has been exposed to parents who, through good intentions or not, have been over-critical. Adam, for instance, had become so tense and anxious about not succeeding that he couldn't perform in a once-favor-ite class. Typically, when such children arrive home and the parent inquires whether there are tests or homework, the child replies an emphatic "No!" A month later the mother may find a pile of such tests under the bed. Often the child is not shirking school responsibility so much as avoiding anticipated criticism. At this age a child, well aware of differences in performance compared with classmates or siblings, becomes extremely sensitive to criticism.

What to Do

1. Examine your own motives for criticizing. Zealous parents who wish to inspire and aid a child's quest for success often frighten by pushing too often and hard.

2. Other parents, assuming the child is lazy, believe they should take corrective punitive action, which worsens the situation.

3. Reduce the pressure upon the child. Try to provide an atmosphere that rewards whatever she can accomplish along the continuum of trial and error that learning any skill or subject requires.

4. Keep in mind that each child is different and has differ-ent abilities. Let the child know that although you prefer the best performance possible, you do love her no matter what happens.

FEAR OF BURGLARS (EIGHT-YEAR-OLD)

Mitchell was a bright second-grader. When told by his mother that his parents would be divorcing, he became quite depressed. Although he lived on the third floor of a well-protected apartment building, he woke up one night convinced that someone had just passed his bed.

"Mommy?" he called.

No answer. And now the shadow on his wall from the streetlight looked just like—the outline of a man waiting near his closet! A burglar must have broken in, waiting to ransack the apartment.

Screaming, Mitchell ran toward his parents' bedroom, where he poured out his fears about the burglar who, he was sure, would return another night even if his father couldn't locate him this time in Mitchell's closet or the hallway or near the locked door.

"There couldn't have been a burglar," his mother insisted. "Nothing's been touched. You must have dreamed it."

To Mitchell, however, the burglar was no groggy vision. The boy was sure he'd seen him, and that was that.

Definition

This problem may manifest as a spatial fear of someone lurking in a particular part of the house, or it may relate to fear of injury.

Symptoms

1. A preoccupation with surreptitious entry that may get acted out in play with toys that involve soldiering or various martial arts (G.I. Joe dolls, swords, guns, camouflage suits);
2. Fear expressed at bedtime;

3. Reluctance to go to bed;
4. Awakening during the night;
5. Distraction about the fear during the day.

Motivation

This fear of imaginary spies or burglars does not usually disrupt a child's functioning. At this age the realization that other people have power to act beyond the child's wishes or control is the "switch" for such fear, to which is added the power of an active imagination. What would be paranoid in an adult merely forms a fearsome world of intoxicating intrigue and high drama to a seven-year-old.

What to Do

1. Discuss practical safety issues with the child who suddenly becomes preoccupied with the possibility of spies or burglars, especially imaginary ones, breaking into the house. Demonstrate the locks or bars on your doors and windows and whatever other security measures you routinely use, such as your child never telling a stranger on the phone that she is home alone.

2. Discuss with the child some actual, specific procedures to follow, should she suspect that someone has entered the house. Use words such as, "If you hear something, come to Mommy's room." The basic aim is to reassure the child that there is no danger while also providing a sense of competence and effectiveness at coping with the fear.

3. Place a night-light in the child's room to help reassure her that no one is lurking there when she awakens.

4. Avoid the external stimulation provided by evening TV shows featuring criminals, break-ins, and other violence.

5. For a fuller discussion of contemporary fears, including criminals who are not imaginary, see Chapter 6.

FEARS OF INJURY (AGES SIX THROUGH TEN)

Billy, a six-year-old boy, was playing quietly in the cellar with his new "workbench." Since his parents had bought him one just like Daddy's, he loved to spend hours tinkering around. One afternoon, however, his mother heard a blood-curdling scream from below.

In total panic she raced downstairs to the basement, where she found Billy crying inconsolably while holding the thumb of his left hand. "What happened? What happened?" his mother cried.

When Billy held up his thumb, his mother could see that the scratch measured all of one centimeter in length! Yet he bellowed "I hurt myself" while the tears streamed down his face.

Definition

For the younger group (about age six), this fear involves an emotional reaction disproportionate to whatever has caused it, whether it be a scratch, splinter, or some other physical complaint, such as heat, cold, or tiredness. These children also fear injuries to parents and may compulsively ask parents' location, even when it's in the adjoining room.

Older children (seven and up), with their greater mobility and independence, fear environmental hazards, both natural (storms, cliffs) and mechanical (cars, trains, construction equipment).

Symptoms

1. Preoccupation with being hurt from routine events and natural hazards;
2. Overstated reactions to minor injuries.

Motivation

Fear of even the slightest injury peaks at ages five-and-one-half through six, a period during which the child still feels the infant's vulnerability to unexpected accidents or illnesses (splinters, pinpricks, stubbed toes, a drop of blood, headache, stomachache).

Although a child like Billy may seem to overreact, this response at his age is thus quite normal. The drama surrounding self-injury is large but will disappear after a year or so as he gains more control over his environment. The exception is the child who reaps so much attention from parents or other important people that he will continue the behavior as long as possible.

The average seven-year-old, by contrast, has acquired physical and verbal abilities to do tasks like apply Band-Aids, hold her breath under water, use tools properly, or inform an adult before a doubtful situation progresses too far. Whereas the average six-year-old jumps right in, a seven-year-old hesitates before acting. Although she does not yet plan ahead, the issues of cause and effect ("If I pull that dog's tail, it'll probably bite me") grow clearer. Various religions have traditionally considered seven as the dawning of the age of reason, the time when children first become responsible in their own and others' eyes for their actions.

What to Do

1. Exaggerated fears of injury will subside by themselves unless a parent is overprotective, insistent, for example, on doing everything for the child or warning her against imaginary dangers from ordinary events.

2. Reassure the squeamish or panicky child without belittling her concern.

3. Warn the child about real dangers of playing around

environmental or natural hazards, like power lines or machinery, parked cars, construction sites, rivers, wells, and ledges.

4. For fears of injury associated with kidnapping, sexual abuse, burglars, urban crime, and war, especially nuclear war, and so forth, see Chapter 6.

FEAR ABOUT THE DENTIST OR DOCTOR

Susan was a beautiful, blond, seven-year-old girl who was very sweet. As one of those "good" oldest children of a large family, she trusted everything said to her. She was also extremely bright.

As part of her medical care, her mother brought her for a routine exam at the dentist's office—an occurrence that had never before caused her distress, so she did not fear it. When the dentist examined her, however, he told her there was a little hole in one tooth that he would clean out with a drill. He also assured her it wouldn't hurt and would end quickly.

Nonetheless, when the drill bit Susan's tooth, she screamed. For years later Susan fought with her mother about returning to the dental office. The combination of pain with deceit had proved too much for her, creating a severe fear of the dentist's chair.

Definition

This is the reaction that develops through a negative experience—or the thought of a negative experience—at the hands of a medical professional. A similar scenario can develop with the pediatrician. Although after the age of three most children do not fear doctors, a traumatic episode with, for example, an injection or vaccination can trigger reluctance to visit the office or clinic.

Symptoms

1. Refusal to visit the dentist or doctor;
2. Whether during a home visit or in the doctor's office: behavior that ranges from mild protest to extreme anxiety, shown by shortness of breath, dizziness, or rapid heartbeat;
3. Anger at, or rejection of, the parent who insists upon the medical or dental appointment.

Motivation

Medical fear related to a negative experience oppresses the child who already senses her lack of control over the environment. Moreover, such fear can endure through and beyond childhood.

In 1985 a group meeting at National Institutes of Health, Bethesda, Maryland, estimated that some 35 million Americans "avoid needed dental treatment until forced into the office with a toothache" (*Journal of the American Dental Association,* July 1985). In spite of better techniques and facilities and emergency equipment and better training of all personnel, the obvious conclusions are that many Americans were traumatized at some point by inescapable dental procedures and that much of this trauma may have occurred in childhood during "routine" exams about which the children were not consulted or fully prepared. Dental care is obviously one of those events that happen because in the long term they are "for your own good," although in the short term they can be messy and frightening.

Fear of the dentist, as of the doctor, can already have developed before age six because the office situation itself may be foreign. The big chair, lights, and scary adults can also disturb the child. If the dentist is sympathetic and willing to play, however, he can make a game of the instruments, both reassuring and entertaining the youngster.

What to Do

1. Try to choose a practitioner who works effectively with children and is honest and patient enough to tell whether a procedure will hurt, how, and when. Consult your pediatrician for a referral.

2. Start dental treatment with your child's baby teeth to accustom her to regular checkups. Healthy baby teeth matter because they prepare the space, through proper formation of muscles and bones, that permanent teeth will occupy. They are also needed to develop proper chewing and speech habits.

3. Teach routine preventive care, especially good nutrition and proper brushing before sleep at night, to avoid a great need for dental work.

4. Like other fears of physical injury, fear of the doctor or dentist will probably subside around age seven, whenever the child can communicate with the dentist and, most important, take responsibility for her own dental health. The exception is a child like Susan, who has sustained trauma.

5. To prevent such trauma from developing into a phobia, do not belittle the child's emotions or pain or transmit your own fears of dentistry. Know that a bad dental experience can also generalize into fear of other doctors.

6. If your child becomes hysterical or uncontrollable, consult your pediatrician for advice or referral to another dentist if a personality clash between child and dentist has occurred.

7. Investigate which dentists in your area use new methods to avoid decay and pain, such as coating the surface of new molars with an antidecay bonding material, or "filling without drilling" (cleaning, filling, and sealing the decayed area without using the drill). The first method obviously aims at prevention, and the second, although controversial, postpones or totally avoids extensive excavation until the child is older and better able to understand what is happening.

8. In a 1986 interview Dr. Heber Simmons, new president of the American Academy of Pediatric Dentistry, advised:

> You can help prepare your child for his first dental appointment by describing the dentist and his work in a way your child can easily understand, by being calm yourself and providing reassurance.
>
> But when a child acts up and is clearly terrified, I just make an appointment for another time and send him home. I tell parents not to say a word about it—kids have the right to a bad day. Usually the next visit goes smoothly.

TYPICAL FEARS OF NINE- AND TEN-YEAR-OLDS

In general, fears decrease as the child's powers to cope with reality, deal with anxiety, and develop effective defenses increase.

Although most fears of these years realistically focus on home situations, school, natural hazards, and neighborhood events (including burglary and other crimes), some ten-year-olds in particular may reexperience earlier fears of the dark, dogs, wild animals, or being left alone. What differs, however, is the child's reaction, compared with the average six- or even eight-year-old confronting the situation. According to Jean Piaget, who spent a lifetime researching the stages of children's thinking as they mature, the ten-year-old has relinquished magic in favor of logical notions of cause and effect, historic and present time, and ability to discriminate size, weight, and volume of objects, including fearsome ones. It is harder to fear something if you are busy analyzing how it works.

Moreover, many research studies of the last twenty years have concluded that rational concern with bodily injury to self or loved ones is a salient fear during middle childhood as ghosts, monsters, and other supernatural creatures recede along with the rich fantasy life of childhood that created them.

Here are typical fears of ten-year-olds and what to do about them:

The dark (dark room or street)
1. Help the child ascertain that she needs to rectify the problem.

2. Offer a night-light or set up another system to keep the child from being alone after nightfall.

3. Initially encourage talking about the fear, but do not dwell on it overlong or it will be reinforced.

Dogs
1. Discuss the fear with the child to ascertain which dogs are fearsome and why (probably size, noise, and unpredictability).

2. Use reasoning and logic to help the child devise action.

Snakes
1. Since this fear rarely interferes with a child's functioning unless she has encountered a snake or heard snakebite stories, use the fear as an opportunity to educate. Find pictures of both harmless and poisonous snakes for where you live or will travel.

Wild animals
1. Follow directions as with snakes.

Heights

1. Since this fear of falling or losing control in high places is a rational one, use it to educate about proper safety precautions around tree houses, towers, cliffs, open windows, fire escapes, or whatever hazards your neighborhood features.

2. Teach your child how to say no to friends engaging in reckless activities.

Burglars, criminals, killers

1. If a child has experienced real violence in the neighborhood, seek professional help for effects of stressful trauma that do not abate within a reasonable time after the incident. (See suggestions in the Fear of Burglars section earlier in this chapter and in Chapter 6.)

2. If a child is generally anxious despite no specific incident, demonstrate the security measures of your house or apartment building to prevent unlawful entry. Use the anxiety to help the child remember to use locks and keys, not to divulge information or display money to strangers, and so forth.

Fires

1. If a child has been injured in a fire, seek professional help for associated psychological trauma that does not remit within a reasonable time.

2. If the child is just generally anxious about the possibility of fire, use the fear to teach proper safety precautions with items like matches, stoves, and heaters, including a strategy for what to do should a fire occur in your home or apartment house.

Being left alone

1. When you cannot be at home, employ a baby-sitter for a ten-year-old, who may state she is old enough to remain alone but does not really believe it.

2. Do not stay at home just because a healthy ten-year-old fears your leaving. Make sensible arrangements to help during your absence—such as turning lights on, giving permission to watch TV, and choosing her favorite baby-sitter.

At the age of ten, fears of wild animals, snakes, and insects may resurface. When asked why she fears snakes, a ten-year-old will easily state "A snake can sneak up and bite you" without questioning whether this event is probable or even possible where they live. In this aspect ten-year-olds thus resemble children much younger, as did the eleven-year-old California girl reported in one of Dr. Adah Maurer's studies ("What Children Fear," *Journal of Genetic Psychology* 106: 265–77, 1965). Although the child was badly burned and scarred in a house fire, when asked "What are the things to be afraid of?" she gave the usual response: "Lion, tiger, dog, cat, snakes, rattlers, spiders."

When some stalwart ten-year-olds boast of the things they categorically do *not* fear any longer, can you guess what these are, according to Dr. Arnold Gesell?

Of course: the dark, dogs, and being left alone—even with wishful thinking!

CHAPTER 5

. . .

Will They Like Me?: Fears of Children Eleven and Twelve; Thirteen Through Sixteen

INTRODUCTION: ELEVEN- AND TWELVE-YEAR-OLDS

Are you surprised to learn that eleven is "the most fearful age"? According to a respected authority, the psychologist Arnold Gesell, that is indeed the case.

For the individual youngster, the reason probably stems from the eleven-year-old's curious status. No longer exactly a child (if puberty has begun) but not yet a teen (with whatever privileges that brings), he is approaching a critical transition.

In October 1985, *USA Today* published the results of Search Institute's poll on the worries of 8,000 ten- to fourteen-year-olds. "The highest percentage of children worry very much about":

Grades	56%	USA violence	36%
Looks	53%	Drugs, drinking	35%

Popularity	48%	Nuclear destruction	
USA hunger,		of USA	25%
poverty	38%		

As youngsters mature into adults, their fears too become better articulated, more realistic, and varied, compared with younger children. Following the organization of previous chapters, therefore, we have arranged this chapter's topics by age groups and by the three major categories of all human fear—natural, personal (including sexual), and social.

TYPICAL FEARS OF ELEVEN-YEAR-OLDS

At this age, fears based in nature or environment involve infection and disease, plus animals and the dark (see separate sections below) and heights (see thirteen-year-old below).

Personal fears involve injections (see Chapter 9); being left alone, especially in the dark; burglary and mugging (see section below on intruders and Chapter 6); plus, in girls, anxiety about being kidnapped (see separate section below and Chapter 6).

Fear about social popularity in school or neighborhood may also characterize eleven-year-olds, especially girls.

FEAR OF BEING ALONE

1. If your otherwise independent eleven-year-old begins to fear being alone, attempt to ascertain what incident might be responsible for this regression. Once the causal factor is determined, take steps to remedy the situation. Sometimes an independent eleven-year-old will just go through a phase of missing the earlier security he knew as a child. Remedy this with a temporary night-light or other measures (baby-sitters, phone calls) to ward off loneliness.

2. Do not, however, let the child return to total dependence on you, since this can terminate in refusal to go to bed and other sleep problems.

FEAR OF INFECTION AND PHYSICAL PAIN

1. Reassure and educate the child about the realistic chances of contracting specific diseases. Since most communicable diseases—other than colds and flu—have become quite rare and diseases like cancer and circulatory ailments typically strike much later in life, this should not be hard.

2. Channel the fear to positively reinforce techniques of proper hygiene, such as dental care and handwashing before meals.

3. Do not join the child by being overly concerned—fearful—of health dangers.

FEAR ABOUT UNPOPULARITY, INCLUDING BEING BULLIED

1. Since social interaction with peers now forms a major part of your child's life, empathize with your child's worries ("That sounds awful. That would upset me, too") without, however, dwelling upon them.

2. Help your youngster learn some skills to remedy worries about friendship or influence on peers—how to choose more trustworthy friends; how to speak up in a group when a decision is being made; how to decide, by weighing pros and cons, whether he really wants to participate in an activity.

3. If bullying by boys is the problem at or traveling to or from school, consult school authorities about effective action. From ages seven through twelve, boys identify strongly with other boys and study their fathers to learn skills needed for manhood. The female playmates of two or three years before, are now foreign entities, and can become victims of what the boys perceive as ways to exhibit their new male bonding.

TYPICAL FEARS OF TWELVE-YEAR-OLDS

These commonly feature heights, creaking noises, intruders, and crowds (for which, see section later in this chapter). As both boys and girls enter puberty, the parent's task involves encouraging the drive toward maturity and independence—mingled as it is with yearning for the security of childhood.

FEAR OF NOISES AND INTRUDERS

1. Know that these are normal fears that should pass as the child matures. He may or may not communicate them to you.

2. If you find your child anxiously investigating locks on doors or windows, say nothing that can damage self-esteem already strained by the child's sense of his own vulnerability in the world.

3. If, however, your child develops an obsession about potential dangers lurking in home or neighborhood, discuss these concerns. Try, of course, to discover whether some troublesome event has actually occurred.

FEAR OF CROWDS

1. Know that what the crowd inspires in the child probably combines a sense of his own vulnerability, danger, and worry about loss of control.

2. Do not embarrass him by ridiculing the feelings.

3. If the fear becomes incapacitating to the point that the child will no longer leave home to attend school or other functions, seek professional help. Fear of crowds can be one symptom of various phobias that include a feeling of being trapped, unable to escape or even breathe. Claustrophobia (fear of enclosed spaces) and agoraphobia (see Chapter 10) are examples.

FEAR OF ANIMALS

Jerry, an eleven-year-old boy who did well in school, had successful parents and many friends. He and his family lived in New York City and had a country home in Connecticut, which they visited on weekends.

One Thursday evening Jerry began having sleep problems. After he finally fell asleep, he awakened several times during the night. On Friday morning he complained of a stomachache and dizziness at school. Because he couldn't attend to his work, his teachers knew something was wrong.

When the Friday evening trip to Connecticut loomed, he froze at the car door. "No!" he screamed. "I can't do it." Clutching his stomach, he began to groan. His parents postponed their trip and consulted their doctor, who found nothing wrong and advised them to leave.

The next day they started on their way with an ashen-faced boy. Not until they entered their house did Jerry reveal his true concern: "It's all the snakes out there." During the previous visit, while he fished in the lake, a black snake—head raised—

had glided toward him until he screamed, dropped his fishpole, and ran.

The fear did not materialize, however, until three weeks later when a new visit to the house loomed.

Definition

Fears of that (by now) familiar category of nature—animals—characterize this age group, as they did the younger child. Often mentioned creatures are snakes, bugs, cows, and bulls.

Any of these fears may be energetically and articulately defended, in contrast to the ten-year-old who may boast of all the things he supposedly no longer fears (such as being left alone in the dark with a bug!).

Symptoms

1. Various physical manifestations of anxiety before or during encounter with the feared object;
2. Vigorous protestations. Some children will instead attempt to avoid the object rather than show, or even discuss, fear.

Motivation (Nature Fears)

The eleven-year-old's fears have a reality-based source in nature or neighborhood. Once imaginary monsters have yielded to specific, concrete animals, the family Oedipal triangle is of less interest than the social hierarchy in school, where rankings of many kinds risk that some children will feel ignored or scorned.

Also unlike younger children, the average eleven-year-old has replaced supernatural magic with an understanding of cause and effect in the natural world.

What to Do

1. Try to ascertain what the child fears.

2. Remember that such dread is real. Help the child learn what to do, should he actually encounter the alarming object or situation. If he says, "Mommy, I'm afraid of snakes," you can answer, "Let's figure out the difference between the harmless and the poisonous ones. You studied them in school. Let's see whether any poisonous ones even live around here."

3. Teach the child appropriate techniques of self-defense so that he will not just stand frozen and helpless before the feared object. We are not authorities on poisonous reptiles, but the usual recommendation on snakes, for instance, is to move gradually out of their way and avoid startling them. More specific help can be found in reference books.

4. Differentiate for the child between psychological fear and the actual, physical encounter.

5. Know that although animal fears may continue to age twelve and resurface at fourteen, if properly handled they will decrease or vanish by fifteen or sixteen.

Indeed, fears of such natural items as large animals, insects, storms, or the dark are the *only* large category of human fear that does decrease as the average human matures, according to a study of nearly two hundred children aged six to sixteen who responded to a fear inventory of sixty items. In their paper "Factor Structure of Childhood Fears" (*Journal of Consulting and Clinical Psychology* 39:2, 264–68, 1972), child psychiatrists Lovick Miller, Curtis Barrett, and others concluded,

The fear of natural events is clearly associated with childhood, and tends to disappear with increasing age or to become focused around the dark and a sense of loneliness. . . . No adult studies report fear of natural events [except for two studies that] report a fear of the dark and loneliness. A fear of bugs and small creatures appears in adult studies as an independent factor, but these are minor items. . . .

The major conclusion is that "fear of physical injury and psychic stress carry through much of the life span, while fear of natural events mitigates with maturation."

FEAR OF KIDNAPPING (ELEVEN-YEAR-OLD-GIRLS)

Mary was an eleven-year-old who lived in a small mountain town; except for some winter ski business, the town was quite quiet. In fact, its sheriff and one police officer spent more time investigating traffic violations and reports of juvenile delinquency and stray dogs than dealing with "crime."

One day, however, Mary heard on television about the kidnapping of the child of a famous fashion designer. From then on she glued herself to the TV evening news, obsessed with the topic of kidnapping. She asked interminable questions of her parents. Next she took a different route to school each day and began personally checking all doors and windows in the house each night.

Motivation

Obsession with this topic is related to simultaneous sensing of growing independence and vulnerability. In girls of this age it probably relates also to the dawning of puberty and sexual feelings, when girls can feel both proud and afraid.

It is sad to say that kidnapping has become of grave concern in today's world. What once existed mainly in children's fantasy is now too often a horrid reality for both girls and boys. Precautions against this tragedy are important.

What to Do

1. Educate your child to protect him from kidnapping by learning "streetwise ways," such as avoiding strangers' offers of money, kittens, or candy or their requests for help in what seems a useful task, such as finding a lost pet or giving street directions. For further information, see Chapter 6.

2. Having done this, try to help your child keep from worrying unnecessarily about the topic.

FEAR OF BEING ALONE IN THE DARK (AGES ELEVEN THROUGH THIRTEEN)

Twelve-year-old Chad was big for his age. He lived alone with his mother, a successful businessperson. Because Chad had shown so many behavior problems for so long, he had been asked to leave three different public and private schools because of refusal to listen to teachers and his perpetual clowning in class.

Furthermore, his bravado penetrated all his actions—except his bedtime habits. Not only did Chad fear the dark; he could not fall alseep unless his mother turned on the light at his bedroom door. The light assured that he could see what he called "the fingers of dark" that he was sure floated or slithered through his door. He, of course, would never admit this to anyone.

Symptoms

1. Refusal to enter a dark room;
2. Excuses to avoid bedtime;
3. Wanting a flashlight or night-light;

4. In serious cases, the classic symptoms of anxiety—rapid pulse, perspiration, dizziness.

Motivation

Although fear of the dark and its noises reemerges at age ten, it can also preoccupy the eleven- or twelve-year-old's mind for various reasons. As adolescence begins, a complex chemical change occurs in the child, characterized by new and increased feelings of sexual tension and aggression. This strange interface of budding adolescence with the final vestiges of childhood creates a curious creature here. Such a regressive dread as that of the dark may also indicate a fear of growing up.

Since all these sensations frighten the child, they can cause various behaviors that otherwise seem inexplicable, of which fear of the dark is one manifestation. Worries about peer situations, such as desires for acceptance and conformity, can also pressure the child, making him anxious at night.

Because the average reality-oriented child of this age feels uncomfortable either admitting to, or coping with, such a fear, certain contradictions may confuse you. For example, the child who no longer tolerates a baby-sitter can be the very one who jumps at noises in the night. Fears may also heighten after some other genuine stimulus, like a neighborhood burglary or seeing a horror movie.

What to Do

1. Don't ridicule the child with admonitions such as, "Don't be a baby." This fear, both real and common, shouldn't be ignored, especially since it can be easily dealt with.

2. Emphasize the child's own coping skills in other areas, which you are sure will soon develop, and also extend to bedtime. Furnish a night-light or overhead light, but gradually reduce its wattage until the child no longer needs it. A wall-switch mechanism to dim a lamp or overhead light will simplify this. Leaving a radio playing may help.

3. Encourage the child to discover his own solutions. That is, avoid the urge to fix everything. Be sympathetic, but know that it is important to let these preteen youngsters work things out for themselves.

INTRODUCTION: THE TEEN YEARS

Adolescence is probably the most difficult life stage through which a human being must pass. It combines the drives and needs of adulthood with the sensibility and vulnerability of childhood—the struggle to burst from parental molds with desperate need for parents. The adolescent's world is one of uncharted areas that he navigates with an equal mix of bravado and confusion.

During this tortuous ten-year metamorphosis, which should result in individuation from the family unit, the teenager's personality is beginning to resemble the adult one that is fast developing. In order to leave the family, the adolescent tries to fashion an identity of his own. This is a more complex task in our society, which has few surviving and definitive "rites of passage" by which elders in ancient (and some contemporary) tribes signify, "Yes, this person is now fully an adult. Childhood is over."

In Western society, perhaps by default, the primary vehicle for transformation therefore becomes identification with friends, the peer group. Yet these same peers can instill fear in both parents and youngsters as the latter confront norms for dress, reactions, sex, and drugs. A child will react to these situations in various ways, depending on how secure he feels and which goals for the future seem crucial.

TYPICAL FEARS OF THIRTEEN-YEAR-OLDS
Although fears of animals, including large dogs, have much decreased, the exception involves snakes. Other fears may surface when confronted with crowds, heights, or the dark.

TYPICAL FEARS OF FOURTEEN-YEAR-OLDS
This is not a fearful age, with the exception of nature worries about deep water or getting lost in the woods, probably because this teen has lost the younger child's bravado and passion for random outdoor games, like playing explorer or "army man."
Social fears involve rejection and applying for work, plus public performance and gossip (see separate sections below).

TYPICAL FEARS OF FIFTEEN-YEAR-OLDS
These fears, again few, involve animals, bugs, heights, (see separate section below), and being alone in the dark. Social fear centers around popularity.

What to Do

Of the ages studied in this book, the fifteen-year-old is the most independent so far, a willing participant in a round of activities that include home less and less. The drama of adolescent life is fully established.

Thus, fear has no major role at this age, compared with the need to establish one's social image.

What to Do

1. Let this youngster work things out for himself, unless your help is sought. If your help is sought, offer thoughtful advice while trying to understand your child's point of view.

2. Remember that the self-consciousness of this age will block any unsolicited advice.

3. Unless a fear infringes upon the child's life, do not reinforce it by emphasis.

4. Seek professional help, however, for any fear that threatens to generalize or become a phobia. See the beginning of Chapter 8.

TYPICAL FEARS OF SIXTEEN-YEAR-OLDS

Although some sixteen-year-olds will continue to fear new social situations, heights, snakes, and being alone in the dark or on a dark street, this age is almost totally autonomous. The only novel fear—inspired, no doubt, by beginning to drive—involves worry about plane or car crashes (see section below).

What to Do

1. Assume that a youngster of this age will depend on a peer group for most answers to problems he encounters.

2. Expect, however, occasional adultlike conversations that narrate a school incident or ask a question, such as, "Were you ever afraid when you had to talk to a group of people (or go to a dance)?"

3. Discreetly use the conversation to assess whether the child truly seeks help with a fear problem. If your advice or help has not been sought in some time, avoid the temptation to rush in and commandeer the situation.

4. Answer with words that are concerned but nonthreatening: "That sounds pretty rough. Would you like to talk about it to somebody who can help?"

PERSONAL FEARS (INJURY, INJECTIONS, HEIGHTS, KIDNAPPING, TERRORIST ATTACKS, CAR AND PLANE CRASHES)

Concerns with injury to self or loved ones continues the worries of the younger child (aged six through ten) in these areas. In general, children (like adults) in poorer areas worry more about injury from crime, compared with children in affluent neighborhoods whose chief worry involves school and social competition.

Here are typical conclusions from one of the largest fear inquiries:

> 9 and 18 years of age reported that supernatural fears were of little concern to this age group. The younger students listed the few entries in this category. Animal fears decreased after 9 years of age and were negligible after 12 years of age. Fears related to safety, school, and natural phenomena were the predominant fears of the 9 to 12 age group. Economical-political, social relations, and personal conduct fears increased during later childhood and were important concerns of adolescents. (H. Angelino, "Trends in the Fears and Worries of School Children as Related to Socio-economic Status and Age," *Journal of Genetic Psychology* 89:263–76, December 1956, summarized in Sally Miller, "Children's Fears: A Review of the Literature," *Nursing Research* 28:4, July–August 1979)

SPATIAL FEAR: HEIGHTS

Maryanne, a charming thirteen-year-old girl from a small town, had a group of friends with whom she enjoyed all the intrigue typical of her age. One Sunday afternoon in October they were walking around when one of the girls asked, "How about going up the church tower to look at the beautiful leaves?" Since it was the height of autumn, the adventure seemed worthwhile. While climbing the narrow stairway to the steeple top, Maryanne clutched the iron railing, however, and fear seized her as she peered down from one window slit.

When she reached the top, her heart beat rapidly; her head was pounding; and she grew dizzy, fearing she would fall. Her fear increased until she couldn't move, and two of her friends had to lead her down the stairs.

Symptoms

1. Sudden awareness of dangerous depth, with simultaneous attraction to the edge or railing;
2. Rapid heartbeat and breathing, feelings of anxiety, dizziness;
3. Freezing to the spot.

Motivation

Like fear of the dark or snakes, fear of heights is an emotion that is phylogenetically predetermined in human beings. During the 1960s experiments with mammals ranging from rats, goats, and monkeys to human babies showed this fear present from birth as day-old animals confronted a "visual cliff." This is a glass sheet, suspended above the floor, partially covered with fabric (taped directly under the glass) and partially open (fabric on the floor a foot below the glass), so that the animal placed on a center board (the cliff) must choose between "shallow" and "deep" sides.

In his book *Fears and Phobias,* British psychiatrist Isaac Marks describes what happened.

> Human infants aged 6–14 months avoided the "deep" cliff side but crawled readily on the "shallow" side of the board. Most human infants discriminate and avoid depth as soon as they can crawl. Fantz (1961) has shown that even infants aged 1–6 months can discriminate spheres from flat circles, which again demonstrates the infant's ability to perceive depth. Fear of a receding edge remains amongst adults on the edge of a precipice, with a feeling of being drawn down and a protective reflex to withdraw from the edge. A similar frightening effect is produced in passengers when a low-flying helicopter skims the edge of a plateau or of a high building.

Originally, of course, such fear served an adaptive function, helping the organism survive by avoiding falls into pits and holes. In the contemporary world, many children and adults still experience it as a fear of injury from falling and a fear of heights.

If it becomes severely incapacitating, it should be treated *before* it develops into a phobia or generalizes to other situations, such as escalators.

What to Do

1. If your child's fear of heights is interfering with his level of functioning, ask whether he desires help of some kind. Because on an outing one does not expect a tower or bridge to produce an anxiety attack in a normal person, this fear often strikes suddenly, embarrassing everybody.

2. If the child desires to reexperience the feared situation to see whether it can be endured without excessive anxiety, assist this but do not force it.

3. If the child has recently had a head injury, cold, or ear infection or is taking any drug known to affect sense of balance, investigate whether the panic attack, vertigo, or other reaction may stem from a temporary inner- or middle-ear dysfunction. Since it is usually reassuring to learn that a disorienting mental state has a logical, physical cause, your pediatrician or an ear, nose, and throat specialist is the person to consult here.

4. If the fear interferes with functioning, seek professional help.

FEAR OF PLANE CRASHES (AGE SIXTEEN)

Sixteen-year-old Alexia never used to have fears. In fact, periodically she'd gotten into trouble for leaving home around midnight to stay out with her friends. She seemed both spirited and courageous.

The summer after her sophomore year she was given a trip to Greece by her parents to see her grandparents. As the time neared, she grew increasingly anxious until she couldn't sleep. Eating became a chore, and she couldn't concentrate on school work.

Finally she realized how much she feared that her plane to Greece would crash.

Symptoms

1. Preoccupation with possible air disaster;
2. Reluctance to get on a plane;
3. Anxiety reactions.

Motivation

During the midteen years, youngsters and their friends learn to drive and are capable of airplane travel without an adult companion. A further theory suggests that the sixteen-year-old, who is now filled with the sexual and aggressive drives of adolescence, fears his impulses and shies away from vehicles, like planes and cars, that can also run out of control.

What to Do

1. Realize that fear of flying is growing more common, as ordinary fear gets reinforced by the real and increased activity of terrorist groups arbitrarily planting explosives on planes. Considering the thousands of uneventful flights each day, however, the chances of disaster striking remain small.

2. If you notice your teenager developing sleep, eating, or concentration problems before a trip, ask whether these are related to it.

3. If this is so, explore the fear without belittling the teenager. Mention one reality, which is the safety records that do exist. With encouragement and the opportunity to talk, the problem usually passes.

4. If the problem persists and disrupts ordinary life, seek professional help and be guided by the results to let the teen make his own decision about canceling the flight reservation.

FEAR OF SEXUAL RELATIONS (AGES ELEVEN THROUGH SIXTEEN)

Jennifer, fifteen, came from a stable, principled middle-class family. Before she met her boyfriend, sixteen-year-old Brad, she had some sexual experience involving kissing and petting. Although she didn't expect to be a virgin when she married, she knew clearly that she would wait until the time was "right" for a true sexual encounter.

Jennifer was, of course, curious about sex. Her more experienced friends described their experiences like adventurous soldiers on foreign soil. Yet she was also concerned and afraid. Since she had a moral upbringing, she didn't want to do anything to hurt or embarrass her family.

Nevertheless, Brad and she were madly in love. Attending football games together, studying together, they became the local "couple of the year." And they were passionate at night whenever they went out in Brad's car, playing sexually until both got very excited, although Jennifer managed to stop the process each time.

Following one date, however, Jennifer became very frightened, ambivalent about what to do. When she was with Brad, everything seemed fine, but when she arrived home, she felt tense and afraid, realizing what poor control she had over herself. Fearing something bad would happen to her beyond the threat of pregnancy, she also feared her parents would discover the situation.

What most terrified her was the sexual reaction of her body, since she didn't know what to do with the feelings of excitement and yearning. Indeed, her body seemed to possess a mind of its own at those times.

Definition

This fear, which involves anxiety and conflicted tension about sexual interaction, has many manifestations, from preoccupation with clothing and hairstyles through reading sexual-oriented magazines to attending parties during or after which sexual relations may occur.

Symptoms

1. Specific worries about normality, popularity, rejection, physical beauty, and sexual performance and the results of such performance (or failure to do so);

   The AIDS (acquired immune deficiency syndrome) scare especially has rendered many teens more conservative in their sexual behavior, including choice and number of sexual partners. Here are strong words by Denise, eighteen years old, about her ex-boyfriend: "I knew he wasn't being faithful to me. I wasn't prepared to take the risk of him picking up AIDS. So I chucked him. I've got a new boyfriend now. It took me a really long time to sleep with him. . . . And I only went to bed with him because I know he's not had many relationships in the past. I've slept with lots and lots of boys. But that's all ended now. Yes, AIDS has really changed me, changed my life."

2. Distraction, secretiveness, or irritability, affecting schoolwork and performance;

3. Possible sudden (and childlike) closeness to the same sex parent.

Motivation

As most parents know, the adolescent has the mind of a child trapped somewhere within the feelings and body of an adult. Dealing with adult issues, like sexual feelings, often leaves him helpless, frustrated, and frightened, despite the fact that traditional moral strictures have loosened and that varieties of sexual conduct, including experimentation with homosexuality, are now considered normal.

A few youngsters boldly venture into the world of sex with minor disruptions to anyone, whereas the majority—male and female—are confronted with what seems a major crisis. Junior-high-school boys, for instance, may be especially bewildered by sexually more advanced girls. "He'd just started working in the cafeteria when somehow girls discovered him and mobbed him," reported one mother about her thirteen-year-old son. And shy high school girls may be terrified by sexually aggressive male juniors and seniors. "I thought he was turning into an animal right before me. All I could do was get out of that car," said one girl about her first sexual near-encounter.

Most teenagers explore sexual feelings and techniques in order to experiment, give physical comfort, or rebel. Only a small percentage experience sexual intercourse, for instance, for the more adult reasons of enhancing communication and closeness between human beings who are already committed to each other.

Although the mores of youngsters seem less inhibited today than ten years ago, especially in urban areas, there is still much ambivalence and fear attached to sexual activity. Beyond concerns about normality and performance, teens rightly worry about pregnancy and sexually transmitted diseases, including AIDS.

What to Do

1. If you sense that a conversation about sex will soon occur between you and your teenager, try to separate out your own emotions and memories first. The shock that most parents feel upon learning or suspecting that a young person is having sexual relations is understandable, but being shocked or punitive doesn't help.

2. The following advice may seem nearly impossible in a parent-child relationship already strained by other issues, but try to be aware and supportive of the teenager's sexual situation and gain his trust. If the youngster is questioning what to do, explain your reasoning as to how you would approach a decision. This involves your attitudes about whatever is happening

—premarital intercourse, homosexual experimentation, worry about disease, or the need for contraceptive knowledge or devices.

As hard as this task is for parents, it is better to listen to what the child is saying, no matter how morally or practically offensive it first appears to you. Refusal to listen risks a permanent rupture just as soon as the young person can make it out of your household. That is, once the teenager discovers— sometimes to his own surprise—that he can get along without you, he will proceed to do exactly that unless you have forged a bond based on the kind of understanding that allows both of you to retain self-respect and some degree of honesty.

3. Assuming your teenager's trust is gained, do not abuse it. If you are asked, for instance, to keep certain information confidential, think twice about discussing it even with your spouse, let alone friends and relatives. Conversations that begin "Your father and I have decided . . ." or "Your aunt thinks you should . . . " are understandably desperate grabs at waning authority, but they seldom work because the child with the problem merely wonders how this enlarged cast of characters got involved anyway.

4. If your teenager has already made a decision about intercourse or contraception, for example, and it is not the one you would have made, keep your temper and resist the urge to lecture, condemn, or punish. Of course, you must make your own values known, keeping in mind that your child does have a mind of his own. If you try to bully your youngster into obeying, the typical result is rebellion. On the other hand, if you try to communicate—that is, listen, and show that you are listening, to what your teenager has to say—you have the chance of getting your views listened to as well.

During the teen years a parent continues to give information and teach values, and should not avoid doing this. But remember that whatever the child has absorbed of parental morality and ethics about many topics, including bodily care and sexual education, was probably learned years ago when you were also busy bandaging stubbed toes, washing grimy knees and grass-stained jeans, and explaining where babies came from and why those two television people under the sheets were breathing so heavily at 8 P.M.

FEAR OF DRUGS

Mimi, a well-dressed, popular fifteen-year-old, was always invited to parties. A cheerleader at all the games, she was also a good girl who loved her parents and wanted never to disappoint them. She thus had definite standards of behavior.

Halfway through the school year, however, she fell in love with Bob, the handsomest boy in her class. Since she had never experienced such depth of attachment before, at first everything seemed a marvelous adventure. Even her parents liked Bob.

Mimi had never experimented with drugs. Although it was always possible to obtain marijuana and even cocaine at parties and sometimes at school, Mimi had never shown interest. Unfortunately Bob, who had such an interest, asked her to do it with him. While they attended a party, he gave her some marijuana. When she refused, he pressured her until she tried it.

Although the sensation seemed pleasant at first, she soon found objects in the room moving in slow motion. As her consciousness spun, she panicked, watching everyone stare at her. With her final bit of self-control, she asked Bob to take her home.

For the next three days Mimi was terrified, fearing she had hurt herself and/or would become addicted. The worst part was knowing that she could not discuss this event with her mother, who would never have accepted such experimentation.

Symptoms

1. Increased distractibility, moodiness, irritability, poor grades, nervousness;
2. Perturbation if a first experience has already occurred, rendering the child sometimes willing to talk with you in however disguised a fashion.

Motivation

Peer pressure and the ready availability of drugs create a special problem for contemporary teens. As with sexual topics, teenagers are simultaneously exposed to drug education programs to help them learn the dangers of random or steady experimentation and to various illusions about the drugs in question. Most often, they connect with a peer group in a way that makes experimentation all but unavoidable.

Parents should learn as much as they can of the realities—instead of myths—about drug amounts, usage, and combinations in their neighborhood or area. Filling children's minds with myths ("Of course, no drugs are available in your school," "I know you'd never touch that filthy stuff," or "One snort will make you an addict") affect the child little, except to tantalize or frighten him further. Although few parents want to see children experiment with drugs, the fact is, many youngsters do.

What to Do

1. Educate yourself on these issues. An excellent pamphlet series for both parents and children is published by the American Council for Drug Education (5820 Hubbard Drive, Rockville, MD 20852; 301 984–5700). Sample titles are "Marijuana and You . . . Myth and Fact," "Cocaine: Some Questions and Answers," and "Alcohol and the Adolescent." A good booklet

room, calmed me down, and excused me from completing this speech. My relief was immense, dampened only by the news of a second speech to be given only a few weeks later. I was terrified! (*Plus, The Magazine of Positive Thinking* 37:1, February 1986)

Fears about popularity, shyness, or academic competition with peers increase around age thirteen. That is, youngsters of eleven or twelve, when fearful, are more apt to worry about the dark, intruders, and large animals.

Definition

Social fears involve awkwardness or anxiety about rejection at school or in social situations or performances.

Symptoms

1. School: various performance anxieties, involving tests, assignments, sports, whatever the teenager feels poor at;
2. School and home: worry about letting the parent down, conflicting desires both to rebel and to satisfy parental pressure about grades or conduct;
3. Disguised reactions, such as appearing "cool" or its opposite—irritability—to hide feelings of vulnerability or inadequacy.

Motivation

Although adolescent friendships are more constant than those of earlier years, they may suffer both breakups and breakdowns, since popularity ratings matter exquisitely. Furthermore, teens fear the power of gossip, social rejection, or ridicule, plus failure to conform to the mores of their chosen

clique, especially to the fashions, hairstyles, slang, and manner-
isms of its leaders. Probably at no time until old age will the
presence or absence of companions again matter so much.
Probably at no time, including old age, will teens again feel
such simultaneous physical and mental awkwardness.

The benefit of such slavish devotion to a group is the cour-
age and skills it gives to the young person whose chief task in
these years is learning how to separate from the home, income,
and life of his family. Indeed, if this process does not happen
successfully for either economic or emotional reasons, the
problems of the teen years can continue well into the young
person's twenties and thirties.

The drawback of group conformity is the teenager's constant
worry that he doesn't quite fit in and will be told so.

Realize that you are shepherding a normal child, although
he often appears or sounds like a visitor from another planet.

What to Do

1. During these years empathy is the key, rather than the
concrete solution to some situation that would work with a
younger child.

2. Listen carefully. Although you needn't get alarmed at
all the teenager says or claims, try to see beyond the grimaces,
irritabilities, or the nonchalant pose to what is really happening.

3. Although some adolescents mimic symptoms ranging
from hysteria to psychosis, many are neither secretive nor sus-
picious of adults and enjoy confiding, especially in the same-
sex parent. If you are fortunate enough to have such a teenager,
try bridge-building responses such as, "Yes. It is tough to know
your friends don't want you in their group. But you know what
happened to me when I tried to join X . . . ?" *Do not* say, "Oh
well, it doesn't matter anyway" or "Your Uncle Eddie's in the
hospital again. Now he's *really* got problems." Although your

teenager may still love Uncle Eddie, the only pain he can feel right now is his own. However, if he remembers nothing else through the tears or depression, he may remember your ability to cope with distress from many directions (financial, work, marital, family) and not sink under it all.

4. Try not to take it personally if the teen rejects your interest, advice, or solutions. Although every adolescent knows he still needs adult support, he would be the last to admit it.

5. If the teenager is often alone and unhappy at home, watch for signs of increasing depression. If sleep, appetite, or school performance are disrupted, if he no longer enjoys previously valued activities, or if aggressive behavior increases, consult your doctor and describe the symptoms. These often define a clinical depression, for which the youngster will need help.

6. It is no secret that suicide is a leading cause of death in teenagers and young adults. Moreover, the rate rose 240 percent from four suicides per 100,000 (1954) to 13.6 per 100,000 (1977). According to Steven Stack, a sociology professor writing in the *Wall Street Journal* (May 28, 1986; Center for Disease Control Statistics), exact rates for 1983 in the different age groups amounted to 1.1 per 100,000 (ages ten through fourteen); 8.7 (fifteen to nineteen); and 14.8 (twenty to twenty-four). The total thus reaches 5,000 young people who succeed in killing themselves every year.

If you suspect that your teenager is contemplating suicide, call your physician for a referral to a psychiatrist or psychologist—or, if the patient is actively suicidal, take him to a hospital emergency room. Although most troubled teens don't kill themselves, do not take a chance with such a possibility.

FEAR OF CROWDS

Peter attended a good private school in New York City. Always quiet, he began staying even more to himself as he turned thirteen. His parents hadn't noticed his avoidance of outings where large groups gathered until his father offered to take him to a football game.

Peter's refusal of the invitation was most unusual. Indeed, never before had he turned down a football game. When his father asked whether he felt all right, Peter answered with banalities.

However, this avoidance pattern soon generalized to outings with friends and school events, which his parents also noticed and could not explain. Although Peter greatly feared being in a crowd, he also feared admitting or showing it. He simply retreated to his room while the fear continued to intensify.

Definition

Fear of crowds, which typically begins at thirteen, can be related to agoraphobia (see Chapter 10) or can presage the uncovering of a schizoid personality disturbance. Most often, however, it occurs as a function of the social concerns of the normal adolescent, who may then confusingly deny or veil its existence.

Symptoms

1. Reluctance to go out with friends;
2. Denial of any motivation to avoid going out;
3. Fear of being out in crowds;
4. Onset around puberty.

Motivation

At this age, avoidance can be an incipient expression of an agoraphobic syndrome but can also represent, more simply, an adolescent's attempt to reconcile his or her feelings about various social pressures. Such pressures—from parents, school, peers, and a budding sexuality—may build until the youngster feels overwhelmed and desires just to withdraw and hide out.

Diagnostically the difference between agoraphobia or an incipient personality disorder and the normal shyness of adolescence relates to how the problem feels to the youngster. The schizoid personality, characterized by general trouble with, or inability to handle, peer relationships, has no discomfort about such symptoms, however. The agoraphobic person experiences sudden, acute panic attacks in situations from which he cannot easily flee, such as on crowded buses or trains. Fear of such attacks is not only recognized but comes to dominate the person's thoughts.

By contrast, the socially withdrawn adolescent simply uses withdrawal as a convenient means to work out whatever conflicts he faces. Of course, social awkwardness may also complicate the situation if the child has been, for example, snubbed, insulted, or ridiculed.

What to Do

1. Use the same skills previously described in this chapter to maintain open, effective communication with your teenager.

2. If the social withdrawal seems to be the normal, pressure-packed variety, just let the youngster know that you are there for him. Don't push, nag, or try to change a youngster's personality at this age. Most teens will achieve their own way to work things out, probably by dropping some previous commitments to concentrate on new interests or friends.

3. If the problem worsens, however, seek professional help.

FEAR OF GOSSIP (FOURTEEN YEARS OLD)

Cary was a stunning fourteen-year-old girl who had been a successful photographic model throughout her childhood, junior high, and now high school years. Since this work provided both money and a fast track start at a glamorous career, her classmates envied her unusual flair.

She had a few good friends, both boys and girls. When one of the boys asked her to go out with him, they attended a movie from which she returned early after no other activity except seeing the show.

Because one of Cary's girlfriends, however, had also wanted to date the boy, her jealousy soon created a problem for Cary, who found herself being rejected by the group. Soon a rumor started that Cary was a "slut." Because this was so wide of the truth, the injustice and pain of the accusation and now constant rumors and glances frightened Cary. Some days she refused to go to school.

Symptoms

1. Preoccupation with what other people are thinking or saying until the condition begins to resemble paranoia;
2. Worry that one is being talked about;
3. Shyness or avoidance of situations where gossip can happen.

Motivation

Because people love to talk about other people, gossip is a favorite pastime the world over. During the process, furthermore, embellishment of the facts can become distortion of them until feelings of powerlessness, helplessness, and injustice overwhelm the victim. The drama of the adolescent world is already so intense that it's hard for a parent to differentiate reality from fantasy as the teenager recounts what has been said or imagines what might have been said.

It is also necessary to differentiate normal reaction to gossip from an incipient paranoid syndrome—the delusion that there is a plot against the teen. Cary's reaction was not unreasonable, but some teenagers may have similar concerns that are unfounded.

What to Do

1. Since feeling understood is crucial to an adolescent, listen to your teen and respond honestly. Say something like, "I hate it when people make up stories about me, but I think it happens to everyone. What do you think you can do about it?"

2. Hear the child's reaction, then state your own. "What do you think about trying it this way?"

3. Resist the temptation to baby the teenager or solve the problem for him. Instead, guide him toward solving it on his own.

The topics covered in this chapter are those commonly afflicting U.S. teens. Here is what teenagers on two other continents fear.

In Senegal more than eight hundred adolescents, many newly enrolled in urban secondary schools away from their tribal villages, were asked a set of open-ended questions, such as, "Do you have fears? How often? Think and try to make a list of everything that frightens or worries you." The ten chief fears concerned school (nearly 30 percent of respondents), safety, health, personal inadequacy, the future, fear of parents (especially the father), supernatural phenomena, animals, natural phenomena (drought), and political events. Girls and children of farmers expressed the most fears, compared with boys and children of high-salaried fathers.

By comparison, secondary students in France registered nearly three times as high on personal inadequacy (composed of items like "being alone at night," "oneself stealing, lying, cheating, misunderstanding"). U.S. students registered high on political fears. (The complete study by Michel Vandewiele, "Fears of Senegalese Secondary School Students," appeared in 1981 in *The Journal of Psychology* 107:281–87.)

CHAPTER 6

· · ·

Danger City, Danger Sky: Fears of Today

Have you ever seen the cartoon of an urban brick wall that reads, "Just because you're paranoid doesn't mean you're not being followed"? A cheerier version is, "Melancholia isn't what it used to be"!

In 1968 when a group of researchers asked children about the eighty items on a fear survey schedule, among the "top ten" fears were some already mentioned in this book—getting poor grades, being sent to the principal, having parents argue. By 1985, for the same item survey of children seven to eighteen years, two new fears had joined the top ten—a burglar breaking into the house and falling from a high place. In *both* lists, however, more than one third of the children feared "bombing attacks—being invaded," placing this item high in the top ten through three decades, despite different groups of children (Thomas H. Ollendick, "Fears in Children and Adolescents: Normative Data," *Behavioral Research Therapy* 23:4, 464–67, 1985).

Another study showed that 80 percent of the children feared being killed or someone in the family dying in an accident—more even than the 75 percent who named the usual "lions, tigers, and snakes" as objects of dread. About 70 percent also feared the following possibilities: the house burning down, being followed by strange people, and being kidnapped.

Some of our fears are thus prompted by the times in which we live. Through television, even young children have seen or heard of the possibility of the world being blown up in nuclear war or by accident; heating up by the "greenhouse" depletion of the ozone layer; or freezing in the nuclear winter that would follow nuclear holocaust. On the personal level, terrorism, muggings, car thefts, and house break-ins have become sufficiently common that no one can avoid thinking of them. In fact, one psychologist at a leading New York private school mentioned that she no longer asks her students whether they have been mugged—only how often. And because divorce now ends 50 percent of marriages, most children worry whenever they hear their parents arguing.

Although everyone fears street crime, how common is it really and why has it so captured the popular imagination? For comparison, you may be surprised to learn that in 1982 nearly 22 million Americans were seriously injured in household accidents. Also in 1982, there were nearly 6.5 million street and highway injuries, plus 46,000 auto deaths.

By contrast, in 1984 crimes of violence against both persons and property totaled about 10.3 million *(Statistical Abstracts of the United States, 1986).* Of this, the actual number of murders was 18,700.

A little arithmetic shows that statistically most people are more than two-and-one-half times (28.5 million, compared with 10.3 million) more likely to be injured at home or on the road than from violent crime, whether urban or rural.

And our guess is that although you now know intellectually that murder is considerably rarer than, say, slipping in the bathtub or crashing your car, this fact makes you no more willing to open your front door at night or walk a dark street alone. Can adults—as well as children, who worry about dinosaurs or wolves attacking—be fearing the wrong things? If so, why?

The answer probably involves the issue of control or, as one psychologist put it, in Maggie Scarf's article "Anatomy of Fear" *The New York Times Magazine,* June 16, 1974), "The next best thing to being master of one's own fate is being deluded that one is." That is, adults *assume* a mastery of objects like high-heeled boots, ice, stairs, bathtubs, stepladders, cars, boats and motorcycles. Therefore, they do not fear these things because they are inanimate and their use is voluntary and (supposedly) controllable, assuming good eyesight and relevant skills.

Street crime, by contrast, seems both random and malevolent. In the words of writer Maggie Scarf (from the same article), "The degree of fear we feel about a potentially harmful event may be linked, primarily, not to the degree of threat (in terms of the probability that it may actually happen to us), nor even to the amount of injury one imagines one might sustain if it did happen, but to the *quality* of the event or situation itself."

Regarding some topics of this chapter, therefore, such as muggings, both adults and children share heightened, if not always realistic, terror. Regarding other fears, however, such as divorce, sexual abuse, or political scares, including threat of nuclear war, youngsters may have more fears than they dare discuss with their parents. Reasons range from lacking the vocabulary or opportunity to air such feelings to reluctance to admit them. That is, on a topic like sexual abuse, everyone can seem tongue-tied because it hasn't or "won't happen here."

Various studies have shown discrepancies between the number of fears reported by children, compared with those items reported as fearsome to children by their parents. For various reasons the parents underestimated both the number and the variety of terrors. As Dr. Arthur Jersild, one of the pioneers of fear study in this century, remarked, "Children harbor many fears as a kind of guilty secret."

We hope this chapter will facilitate further discussion between you and your child on topics such as sex and politics that, along with religion, once were unmentionable.

FEARS ABOUT DIVORCE

As a therapy group of five boys, all about ten years old, was assembling for its weekly meeting, one boy arrived distraught. When Dr. Schachter remarked, "Jonathan, you look all upset today," the boy burst into tears.

"I just found out my parents are getting divorced," he spluttered between sobs.

"That's terrible," said one little boy. "I know exactly what that's like. My parents did that last year."

Immediately three of the boys—all sons of parents already divorced—crisscrossed their arms about Jonathan's shoulders. "We know what that's like. Let's talk about it," said one. After all, Jonathan was their buddy, and buddies stick together in this uncertain world.

When Dr. Schachter asked Jonathan, "What's the scariest thing about your parents divorcing?" the boy answered, "I don't think I'll ever see my dad again, and I know he's very mad at me."

Another boy said, "Well, I felt like that, too, when my parents got divorced. But let me tell you what really happens. First of all, your parents won't be fighting anymore. Second, you see your dad more because he's not always out. And, third, you get a lot of presents. It's really not so bad."

The rest of the story? Finally Jonathan wiped his tears and began to recover. He and his father shared a number of office sessions to discuss the boy's many questions and feelings about losing his family, especially the reality of his father's leaving. When Jonathan asked whether his father was angry at him, the answer was that he wasn't, of course. The parents did divorce. Although his father moved from New York to Philadelphia, Jonathan did see him frequently. Furthermore, after talking out his loss and anger at the situation, the boy felt much better.

Definition

The fear of divorce has two aspects, depending on whether the child is imagining the possibility of divorce, based on parental behavior, or actually enduring the reality of divorce. Most children will fear separation or divorce whenever they hear parents arguing. This fear touches children of happy marriages as well, since these couples also share differences at varying volume, which a child may misinterpret.

Divorce, whether real or imagined, terrifies the child, since the security of home is invaluable to her sense of well-being. When asked "If you had one wish, what would it be?" during psychotherapeutic evaluation, even adolescents from a divorced home answer, "For my parents to get together again." Indeed, one fifteen-year-old boy gave exactly this answer, despite the fact that his parents had not only divorced five years before but had been remarried to other people for some time.

Divorce, although necessary in many situations, nevertheless remains one of the most devastating experiences a child can endure. Although a parent feels guilty about having to leave a child, there are a few ways to lessen the ultimate impact of divorce.

Symptoms

1. After her parents have an argument, a reticence in the child, who may also vegetate in front of television or hide in her room, turning the music up loud;
2. Often endearing attempts to get the parents to cease fighting, such as running into the middle of an argument, offering to contribute money or to do chores if the fight involves finances or housework;
3. Sleep problems;
4. Change in school performance;
5. Fantasies of terrible things to come—that the child

won't be loved, won't see the departing parent again, can't trust the remaining parent to handle the war of words, blows, crises, or whatever else is happening.

Motivation

For a child of any age, the divorce process entails several discreet stages, similar to those that occur when someone dies. First comes denial—disbelief that such a thing is occurring. The next phase involves guilt, since the child wonders whether she is to blame or feels that in some ways he can keep the marriage intact through proper behavior or by getting the father to listen to the mother.

The third phase is anger at both the situation and the parents. The final stage is resolution—some measure of acceptance in the child's mind as she realizes the parents must work through their differences and make choices based on adult issues. As one eleven-year-old girl said of her parents, "It hurt me in the beginning, but I figured out I couldn't do anything about them."

It is no accident that these stages marking death of marriage parallel Elisabeth Kübler-Ross' psychological stages for an individual's grieving.

What to Do

For imagined divorce:

1. See whether you can relate any of the above symptoms to increased arguing at home or other tensions.

2. Reassure the child with words like, "Mom and Dad have differences sometimes, but we're grown up and know how to work those things out. And we always do work them out. You needn't worry." Or, "Sometimes you shout at your friends. But the next day you play with them again, isn't that right?"

3. Try not to let children into the middle of your arguments. Although many parents allow this because it is tempting and flattering to have a child on your side, it gives the child a power that proves illusory when she discovers the situation cannot be changed by such manipulation.

4. If you have a household where arguments take the form of "cold war"—sullen silence and depression—instead of gales of words that blast through and then vanish, realize that what your child senses most is lack of love from adults constantly wrapped in their own problems. This is a home where tension can be pervasive but its cause elusive, since parents who fear or despair of discussing issues with each other probably won't discuss them with the child either, except in misguided attempts to get the child "on their side."

For actual divorce:

1. Stress that whatever the child may overhear involves adult issues that the child has no part in and should not blame herself for.

2. Reassure the child that both parents still love her, and make some time—despite your own pain—for the child to air her own feelings. "Sometimes this kind of situation makes you feel a lot of things, sad or mad. Let's try to talk about the things that are scary, too." Be careful, however, not to blur your own feelings into the child's, since her experience necessarily differs from yours.

3. Refrain from making yourself appear such a victim of your spouse's bad behavior—malevolence, abuse, stupidity—that your child will wonder whether she can depend on you. Such pleas for sympathy, while tempting, damage you and your authority in the child's eyes.

4. Refrain from those equally tempting, but insulting, stereotypes that occur so easily to the fatigued mind. "Men are all like that," "Women always get hysterical," "Catholics (or some other religious group) are so rigid," "Everybody in his family is crazy, anyway," and so forth. Such words not only make you look poor for having married this now-repulsive person, but they prejudice your child toward whatever group you have criticized. Remember that children at certain ages are themselves rigidly logical. Your child may not understand when, after the divorce, you begin again to date another member of whatever group you have maligned.

5. For the departing parent: Try not to spoil (or buy) the child with expensive gifts to compensate for your absence. Your chief challenge is not to deplete your bank account but to achieve the same, or an even better, relationship while your child visits your new home. An endless menu of gifts is not a realistic way to do this. They may even confuse the young child trying to adjust to the new situation.

FEAR OF PERSONAL INJURY: MUGGING AND NEIGHBORHOOD SAFETY; SEXUAL ABUSE; TERRORIST ATTACKS

Timothy, ten years old, was a rather thin but sturdy boy who lived in a fashionable New York neighborhood. After leaving his school bus one afternoon, he was approached by two older boys who were strangers to his neighborhood. Immediately they blocked his way—one standing behind, the other in front of him. Next they ordered him to give them his money, his watch, and his gold-rimmed glasses.

Although Timothy obliged them, the bullies shoved him to the ground and ran off.

When he arrived home, he was shaking. Since neither parent was home yet, Timothy phoned his mother and cried hysterically. For several weeks he grew dizzy and nauseated as the school bus approached his stop.

Slowly, as time passed, however, his symptoms and fear decreased.

Definition

This fear, shared by both adults and children, involves recurrent and maximum discomfort upon returning to wherever the violence or assault occurred.

Symptoms

1. Extreme, but usually temporary, fear following an actual incident;
2. The victim's irrational tendency to blame herself;
3. Occasional embarrassed refusal to admit fear, particularly in teenagers;
4. Refusal to return to school;
5. Periods of agitation, including sleep or eating difficulty;
6. General decrease in fear level with the passage of time, although one incident may generalize to fear of all subways, buses, stairways, dark corridors, and the like.

Motivation

Anyone who is mugged or injured in a street crime or illegal entry into her home feels, beyond the immediate pain of the assault, a turmoil of fear, anger, violation, and vulnerability within herself, plus the malevolence of the perpetrator. Although everyone fears such events, the child victim, who lacks adult skills even in ordinary situations, feels extra vulnerable and disturbed because of it. Following such an incident, certain youngsters may also feel shame or embarrassment (because they did not defend themselves better) or guilt (if they were injured or robbed while out late or doing another activity forbidden by a parent). Depending on their internal defenses, some may also deny they were afraid at all, but a wise parent would refuse to believe this.

In general, children who have been better prepared can be expected to fare better if an incident occurs. To protect himself and learn better survival skills, for instance, one junior high school boy began hanging out with a tougher group of twelve- and thirteen-year-old boys, compared to his usual friends.

Here are some results to a questionnaire sent by the parents association of Trinity School, New York City, a private interracial and interreligious school for grades kindergarten through twelve. It shows how or when other parents both set limits and teach sexual and street safety without appearing morbidly overprotective.

Although Trinity students run daytime errands alone and use public transport by the ages of eight or nine, all the parents who answered the questionnaire set curfews for children in fourth through eighth grades—usually "when it begins to get dark." Children in grades five through twelve, although allowed more freedom of schedule, were nevertheless expected to communicate often with parents, especially to discuss changes of plans.

When asked "Have you discussed with your child the specific dangers he or she might encounter, especially muggings and sexual advances?" the parents replied as follows. With kindergarten and first-grade children, 33 percent and 46 percent of parents had discussed such subjects. In the second grade, 63 percent; third grade, 79 percent; fourth grade, 94 percent; fifth grade, 89 percent; sixth grade, all students; seventh, 83 percent; eighth, 96 percent; ninth, 88 percent; tenth, 96 percent; eleventh, 96 percent; and twelfth, all students. These parents were trying hard to provide guidance, just as they already had done about other basics like safety around animals, street crossings, or hot stoves.

Detective Jack Meeks, of the New York City Police Department's Crime Prevention Section, organizes school safety presentations for kindergarten through third-grade groups. He recommends, "The time for teaching safety measures is when children are young. Children should learn how to handle themselves while they are in the first few years of school. Then by the time they do go out alone, they will have developed their instinctive security know-how."

What to Do

1. Begin by discussing traffic safety while you and your child observe traffic lights, cross streets, and so forth.

2. Use the inevitable incidents that television provides— car chases, holdups, assaults, terrorist bombings, and so forth —to ascertain and discuss those fears your child already has. These can take the form of, "If that ever happened to you or me, what would (should) we do?"

Indicate in your own words that since many perpetrators who perform these desperate acts are far from sane, the best course of action is to try to keep your head and not anger or alarm anyone who has trapped you and is waving a weapon.

3. Emphasize that, out in the street, children's usual rules of polite behavior toward adults need not apply. Regarding strangers, a child can learn to ignore questions, say no, walk away, refuse to do a task, cry or make a scene if someone is following or pestering, refuse offers of a ride, money, kittens, jewelry, dolls, toys, and so forth. The normal adult, for example, does not ask a young child for either directions or the time.

4. The book *How to Raise a Street-Smart Child, The Parent's Complete Guide to Safety on the Street and Home* by Grace Hechinger (Fawcett Crest/Ballantine, New York, 1984) contains excellent sets of what-if questions (with answers) that you can transmute into a safety game or test with your child. Samples are: "Your mother gave you some money to buy an ice cream cone. On the way to Baskin-Robbins, a bigger boy asks for money and threatens to hit you if you do not give it to him" and "You are in a park, and a man walks up to you and says, 'Please help me find my dog. He's disappeared, and I can't find him.'"

5. Although you cannot personally protect your child against every situation she will encounter, calmly discussing events like these will increase both her self-confidence and street skills and—most important—provide the vocabulary to confide potentially harmful or violent events, should they occur. After all, you can't prevent the worsening of a situation that your child, lacking preparation and fearing your punishment or blame, initially feared to tell you.

6. Show your child how to use the 911 emergency telephone number.

7. YMCAs, YMHAs, and martial arts schools throughout the United States now give various self-defense courses for both young and older children (ages nine and up). Because a child is not sufficiently strong enough to fend off attack by teenagers or adults (or sufficiently motivated to practice regularly), small children should not be encouraged to defend themselves this way. However, the courses do teach valuable bodily discipline and mental self-control (how to keep one's head in an emergency).

8. As with most of the other fears mentioned, too much emphasis or attention can foster the fear. A realistic attitude which is sensible and not overly worrying seems best.

FEAR OF SEXUAL ABUSE

Every Sunday nine-year-old Carrie visited the candy and newsstore in town just before the afternoon movie. Since her parents, too, stopped there for newspapers and other items, Carrie had no reason to fear its newest employee, Mr. O'Donnell, a man about fifty whose grown daughters she knew and who even served as church usher. Indeed, in his white shirt, tie, and suit he resembled her father.

One Sunday after the other children had rushed to the theater, he invited her to the store's back room, promising a special toy. Indeed, she'd already been back there with other employees in search of stock items. All he had to show her, however, was a silly mechanical cow whose udders he filled with water and "milked" with his black mechanical pencil. Noticing her boredom, he told her she could read any magazines and comic books she wanted—free—and pick out her favorite and he'd give it to her. Having chosen a Wonder Woman comic, Carrie left for the movie.

Next Sunday when she returned in her best two-piece dress and they were alone, he began to touch her chest and between her legs, at first through the clothing and then underneath it. When one of his lighted cigarettes touched her white piqué collar, he helped her unbutton her jacket and wipe away the ash marks before her mother saw them. Next he unzipped his trousers and exposed himself. Puzzled, she stared at him, then left the shop. Nor could she figure out, in the days between visits, the reason for his intense interest in her. Although she did well in school, she knew her mother considered her awkward and skinny and her father always seemed busy and exhausted by his job.

Despite her determination not to return, a few weeks later with both parents napping from the rigors of a week's work and a large Sunday dinner, Carrie felt lonely and again visited Mr. O'Donnell. This time in the back room he unzipped his pants and pressed himself to her. She felt something hard.

Terrified at this strange event, Carrie screamed, squirmed, and tried to run, but his large hands caught and stroked between her legs, inside her underpants, and across her chest. He seemed to be comforting her, which again confused her. Although half of her wanted to scream and run, the other half knew he seemed far more thrilled by her than either of her parents, despite the fact that she was an only child.

When he had calmed her, he warned that they were playing "grown-up games even your mother won't tell you about," which was true, since her mother had told her only the facts of how babies got born with nothing about preliminaries and even less about emotions. And since her father had said nothing on such topics, she doubted he knew anything at all. "Don't tell anyone" were Mr. O'Donnell's last words as he helped her straighten her dress.

Badly shaken, she dashed from the shop to her favorite cave in the woods, where she cried and blamed herself for letting him do all that stuff.

Several weeks later she was relieved to see he no longer worked at the store. But it was two years before she discussed the incident with her best friend and fourteen years before she told her mother. When she married at twenty-five, she found herself terrified at the thought of pregnancy.

Motivation

Sexual abuse is a wide-ranging and recurring topic, depending upon your child's age, gender, and other variables, but the parent's first step should be correct information instead of myths. According to studies quoted in various sources, including *No More Secrets: Protecting Your Child from Sexual Assaults* by Caren Adams and Jennifer Fay (Impact Publishers, San Luis

Obispo, CA, 1981), most sexual abuse does not result from one isolated incident or violent attack by some weird or dangerous stranger. As with Carrie, such offenses (1) are usually committed by a person whom the child knows, including relatives, family friends, or store or building employees; (2) happen gradually and repeatedly, taking various forms as time passes and the child does or does not cooperate; and (3) employ subtle, rather than explicit, force, especially bribery, flattery, or threats to the lonely, upset, or friendless child, especially the one who is feeling unwanted or unloved at home. The child who has self-esteem is less likely to be victimized.

It should always be remembered that sexual abuse is an issue for the parents of boys as well as girls, and is found in all strata of our society. As one father remarked to us, "It used to be you worried only about daughters. Now you have to worry about sons, too." Here are some results of a recent study of 122 now-adult men who were sexually abused in childhood (reported by Felice Lee in *USA Today,* February 26, 1985). The two chief conclusions were that most sexually molested boys never reported it (only 3 of the 122 told anyone) and that they still refuse to label the experience as abuse. Although this sounds as if it had little impact upon them, read these further statistics:

- 75 percent reported "fear, confusion, anger, and resentment" after the incidents;
- 20 percent reported the abuse "had a negative impact" on their later sexual performance;
- 20 percent had fantasies about sex with children.

The most surprising discovery? Seventy-five percent of the abusers were female—family friends or relatives. The point here is not whether the incidents were heterosexual or homosexual. The problem is how to protect children from the "love" of lonely, malfunctioning adults.

What to Do

1. Provide your child with proper sexual education, including terminology such as "penis," "vagina," "breasts," and some way to describe sexual feelings. To discuss sex honestly without embarrassment, you and the child need words more accurate than "down there." Begin with an anatomy drawing in an encyclopedia or dictionary if you are stuck for some nonpornographic way to present information.

2. Remember that a child's first experience of sexual feelings is apt to involve masturbation, which she will do more or less openly, depending on your attitude. Use this, plus your child's spontaneous questions about babies, pregnancy, intercourse, the difference between the sexes, and similar matters, to begin some kind of discussion. Say something like, "Your sexual feelings are normal and natural, but it takes a long time before a young person can learn or do all the things that caring for a baby and a home require."

3. Do not indicate that your child is somehow bad for wanting to discuss sexual topics, including sex-related worries with you.

4. Warning a child against "strangers" is no adequate preparation against sexual abuse, since "strangers" do not commit most of it.

5. Teach your child about "body zones," that certain parts of our bodies are off limits except for medical exams by doctors or nurses, and that although certain touches make us feel good, they too should be off limits except later in life, to people who actually love and care for each other. If your child cannot learn something about the value of sexual intimacy within your marriage, for instance, she may learn some worse version of it elsewhere.

Stress that "private parts are private parts"—except when revealed in love or for some valid medical reason.

6. Teach your child that she can say (at the first intuition of some odd situation), "Stop," "No, that's enough," "Don't do that," and—very effective—"I'm going to tell." Warn your child against anyone who uses phrases like "secret games just between you and me" or "all-boy games between us men." Such language is very tempting to children, unless they know the person is using it for selfish, abnormal purposes. That is, many male sex offenders are unable to function normally with their wives or women or men of their own age; hence their interest in the easier targets that children present.

7. Teach your child that she can run away without explanation, that this person does not deserve answers to questions, thanks for help given, or whatever respect a child usually renders an adult.

POLITICAL FEARS, ESPECIALLY FEAR OF NUCLEAR WAR

Eight-year-old Melissa was participating in a therapy group of four girls to help her with some social difficulties. One day while the girls discussed fears they had, Melissa surprised the therapist by saying that her most profound fear involved nuclear war. As other members discussed the question, they too mentioned nuclear war. Each of these young girls was extremely frightened that a war might occur and, if it did, they and all they loved would be destroyed. These thoughts dominated each of their minds at different times.

The therapist noted that although their economic and religious backgrounds differed, the children were all middle class, without parents involved in antiwar activism of any kind. Their fear therefore seemed to be a direct, pervading kind that could not be explained by parental differences or "special coaching."

Definition

Fear of nuclear war involves an underlying, pervasive concern that may or may not be expressed, depending on the child's personality and the situation. Although children will usually discuss fears of nuclear disaster when asked, they—like adults—ordinarily lack a forum in which to do so. Although this does not affect most children's level of performance, it is a factor for parents to consider when evaluating possible extra pressure that a child faces.

Symptoms

Possible periods of restlessness, distraction, or irritability, especially following television programs or school discussion on nuclear themes or parental statements of horror or despair about nuclear issues.

Motivation

Although predictions of the end of the world have always afflicted one or another social group, depending upon its location, food supply, or religious beliefs, what is new in "futurology" is its global scale on issues like overpopulation, famine, and environmental destruction. The 1986 meltdown at the U.S.S.R.'s Chernobyl reactor demonstrated how vulnerable neighboring countries and the whole world, regardless of political ideology, are to nuclear death and disaster.

Here are a few comments—tragic because they have become typical when normal children try to imagine the effect of nuclear war:

When I was very young, seven or eight, I did not know what the dream was at the time. I first felt intense fear, complete and utter destruction. This dream came back throughout my childhood, and it wasn't until five or six years ago that I figured out that this dream was a nuclear holocaust. Thinking of this scares me more than anything I've known yet. (Boston teenager)

Why is this called the happiest time of our life? I have a lot of worries and so do my friends. . . . Suppose there is a nuclear war. Suppose the air gets polluted. Suppose there isn't any gas left when I grow up, if I get to grow up at all. I wonder why we go to school and work so hard if it's all for nothing. Some of my friends do drugs and drink because they say they aren't going to last anyway, so why not? (Letter to advice columnist; both quotations from the *American Journal of Orthopsychiatry* 52:4, 592, 1982—part of a set of articles on children's perceptions of nuclear war)

The following sentences are from *What About the Children?*, one of the excellent pamphlets published by Parents and Teachers for Social Responsibility (Box 517, Moretown, VT 05660):

Experts have studied both the short- and long-term impact of the Hiroshima-Nagasaki bombings. They tell us that the survivors who suffered most were babies, children, the aged, the sick, and the handicapped. In short, those most in need of strong family support.

Here are a few research results on reactions of children of various ages and nationalities to the threat of nuclear war. We chose the ones that begin with unbiased questions, such as "When you think about the future, what three things do you most hope for?" and "What three things do you most worry about?"

In 1965, when S. Escalona asked three hundred fifty U.S. youngsters how the world might be different in ten years—

without mentioning nuclear war—70 percent spontaneously mentioned the bomb, nuclear war, or a destroyed world. In newer studies (1978 to 1980) by W. Beardslee and J. Mack, when 1,151 students in grades 5 through 12 from urban and suburban Los Angeles, Boston, and Baltimore were asked ten questions on topics ranging from nuclear attack to blackmail by terrorist groups, half the sample proved aware of nuclear issues before age twelve. Typical figures showed that 70 percent of girls and 50 percent of boys believed that radiation from nuclear wastes and power plants would shorten their lives ("The Impact on Children and Adolescents of Nuclear Developments" in Psychosocial Aspects of Nuclear Developments, Task Force Report No. 20, American Psychiatric Association, Washington, DC).

Again in the United States in 1980, J. Goldenring's and R. Doctor's study, "Adolescents' Concerns About the Threat of Nuclear War," surveyed 913 junior and senior high students in six California schools about twenty possible worries. Seventy-four percent stated "my greatest worry" was a parent dying from any cause, and number two in frequency of mention was nuclear war (*Congressional Record,* Testimony before House of Representatives Select Committee on Children, Youth, and Families, September 20, 1983).

Results from other countries are similar, although in areas of high unemployment, like Great Britain, the issue of jobs equally occupies older children's minds. In Finland in 1983, 6,800 students aged twelve through eighteen were asked open-ended questions about the future that did not mention war or peace. Seventy-nine percent of twelve-year-olds and 57 percent of eighteen-year-olds first mentioned fears about war (T. Solantaus et al., "The Threat of War in the Minds of 12–18-year-olds in Finland," *Lancet* 1984 i: 784–5).

In Bristol, England, a 1984 survey asked the same set of questions about hopes and fears of 409 children between the ages of eleven and sixteen. Twenty-eight percent would "ban nuclear weapons" while an additional 12 percent mentioned "making peace" and "stopping the fighting."

In a similar 1984 study of more than two thousand Ontario, Canada, students in grades 7 through 13 (including some immigrant groups), "nuclear war was the most frequently mentioned spontaneous worry and most frequently mentioned first worry." Moreover, and in slight contrast to the British study, "those who are most concerned about the threat of nuclear war are also most concerned about their own future plans." That is, "those who said they had not felt fearful and anxious also expressed the strongest feelings of helplessness," whether about getting a job or preserving the world. They showed "the least interest in planning their own personal futures" (S. Goldberg et al., "Thinking About the Threat of Nuclear War: Relevance to Mental Health," *American Journal of Orthopsychiatry* 55[4]:503–12, October 1985).

We have summarized all these studies because, in the flurry of discussion over apparently more immediate issues like jobs, the national debt, AIDS, and other medical and financial issues, little attention is paid to the ultimate cost of the arms race or the emotional effect it has on all of us, especially the young.

And it is the children who, having the least power, worry most about separation from loved ones and about dying, either by being vaporized or left helpless.

What to Do

1. Explain to children who question that no one wants to start nuclear war, that every country seeks to protect its children. Your task is to help lower your child's anxiety level.

Nevertheless, achieving nonviolence among nations is similar in challenge and nature, if never in scope, to nonviolent solutions to children's quarrels. An excellent article that teaches methods of compromise amid conflict for children's affairs is Judith Myers-Walls' "Nuclear War: Helping Children Overcome Fears," *Young Children* 39(4):27–32, May 1984.

2. Stress that the prospect of nuclear war is one more area of life that everyone must face despite numerous fears, both real and unreal. It becomes another topic where surrendering to fear is as useless as never considering the topic at all.

3. Learn some facts about nuclear escalation. Besides Parents and Teachers for Social Responsibility, there is Students Against Nuclear Energy (SANE) (711 G Street, Washington, DC 20003) and a dozen other active groups.

4. Politically motivated parents have the option to get involved in various ways and the right to educate their children on these issues. The challenge here is how to achieve this without further frightening or worrying children. Ideally, the example of politically aware or active parents encourages a youngster's optimism about the future and faith in individual and collective effort.

5. Avoid making your child a political activist, enlisting her in what will appear to be "your" work. If she desires such commitment, it should be a mature choice to be made later.

SUMMARY

Do you sometimes feel—on a bad day—that you and your children live in a city of criminals, a country of scofflaws, or a world out of control? Do you ever yearn for a supposedly simpler past?

Here are samples of what a few famous cities were truly like —before such modern inventions as street lighting, traffic and animal control laws, not to mention police and fire departments. In ancient Rome "if rich party-goers stepped into the streets, they did so protected by slaves who carried torches to light them on their way." Later in Europe:

Especially for small children, streets in medieval towns were full of hazards, not so much from wheeled traffic as from the large number of animals more or less on the loose. . . . In late medieval times, city councilors issued ordinances to control the movement of swine, but with little success. Galloping horsemen trod children underfoot. All kinds of accidents could and did occur from a traffic that was almost totally unregulated.

In 1765 four Boston newspapers introduced the novel European idea of attempting to harness traffic by having everyone keep to the right on the narrow roads to prevent the following:

Back and forth through the streets coursed horsemen, gentlemen's chaises and chariots, a variety of tumbrils, carts, trucks, and great wagons drawn by from one to eight horses or oxen . . . plus numerous laborers pushing wheelbarrows and countless porters carrying parcels large and small. Everywhere children died under hoofs and wheels; nor were their elders spared by galloping horsemen, reckless carters, or racing gentlemen. . . .

Regarding crime, the eighteenth-century novelist Henry Fielding, who was also a court judge, wrote of London: "The innocent are put in terror, affronted and alarmed with threats and execrations, endangered with loaded pistols, beat with bludgeons, and hacked with cutlasses." One suburbanite complained that he couldn't return home "without danger of a pistol being clapt to my breast. I build an elegant villa, ten or twenty miles distant from the capital; I am obliged to provide an armed force to convey me hither." (All quotations in this summary are from Yi-fu Tuan, *Landscapes of Fear*, Pantheon, New York, 1979.)

PART II

·

· Phobias ·

·

CHAPTER 7

· · ·

"Hell No, I Won't Go!": School-related Phobias

SCHOOL AVOIDANCE

On a morning in your household when the alarm clock fails, the toast burns, and the last thing you need is another problem, has this ever happened?

Sara Rogers stared in disbelief at her ten-year-old son. Usually up at dawn to watch TV cartoons or play with his Go-bots, Jason now clung to his bed, pounding his pillow and kicking. "I won't go. School's gross," he yelled. "Miss Barto's dumb."

"You just had too much Christmas, that's all. Time to get back to work now." Sara sighed. It was five to eight, and she'd be late herself if Jason didn't move soon. If only Frank would help more, but when he did help in the morning, it was usually locating shoes and underwear for the younger Susan. If only Mama could have lived a little longer—

Sara leaned to feel Jason's forehead and cheeks. Hot and red from exertion, she guessed, not fever. "Jay, you have to go to school."

"I do not. I told you last week. How Miss Barto's a—bananahead. I wanna stay home with you." Seated now on his bed, Sara tried to hold his hands and hug him, but he pulled away. "I won't bother you. I promise."

Frank stuck his head into the room. "C'mon, Jason, get up. Don't make Mama late for her appointment."

"I'm *not* going." In ten more seconds Jason lay in tears.

In her own words Sara remembers. "I called the school, but they said he was doing fine with his work, that kids were hard to settle down anyway, after the holidays. The principal suggested I call the pediatrician. When I told him I couldn't get Jason to school short of chaining and dragging him, she didn't believe me. I felt like a fool, but I canceled my appointment and let him play in his room while I drove Susan to her day care.

"Next morning was even worse. After protesting again about school, he threw up his breakfast on the bedroom floor. The next two weeks were a nightmare, either a fight or vomiting every morning. His teacher was stumped, too. She said attendance problems are common with three- and six-year-olds who still want Mom, but not with a fourth grader like Jay. When the pediatrician found nothing, not even a sniffle, she did ask, 'Jason, are you upset about something?'

"When he stared away, frightened and guilty, she couldn't get more from him. She suggested a psychologist. Meanwhile I kept making excuses to the school. Although he'd always been close to my mother before she passed away, I certainly encouraged him to confide in me, too. What could make his sudden fear of school?"

At first the psychologist found Jason hyperactive and hyperexcited, willing to talk about anything but what was truly troubling him. Gradually from the parents he got a full history of major life events, including the most recent and crucial—the maternal grandmother's death from a heart attack two months before. The mother added, "It upset all of us, but she and Jason were especially close. He was her special little boy."

Encouraged to talk about Grandma, Jason at first enthusiastically described all the activities they'd done together, and her prowess at cooking, baking, storytelling. Next he dissolved into tears when he began to describe her funeral. "I know Grandma's dead, but why does she have to stay dead so long?" he sobbed. "Now I'm afraid Mama will leave, too."

Meeting together, the psychologist and Jason's parents agreed on short- and long-term goals for his care. The immediate, obvious goal was to return him to school; the long-term, to help him cope with grief over his grandmother. A bargain was struck with Jason and the teacher. If he would attend classes the next day, his mother would stay for early morning, and he could come home at noon. This worked; both parents praised him; and by the second week, Jason's mother merely left him at the school entrance. By the third week, he was going alone as usual.

During this time Jason and the psychologist met twice weekly. To control his fear, the little boy was taught deep breathing and progressive muscle relaxation exercises to use when approaching the school building. When asked to tell stories about and rank school events from least to most frightening, Jason named arithmetic, the kids who ridiculed and wouldn't play with him, and the teacher yelling at him. He then mimicked how silly the teacher looked while yelling.

Now past the crisis, Jason had group play therapy (see the Afterword) and joined his parents for a monthly family therapy session, all aimed at helping him verbalize his feelings and learn better ways to express anger. After one play session one of the boys mentioned how he felt about a sick parent. Jason spoke up, "I felt that way when my grandmother died." His face crumpled as he wiped at tears.

As when Jason had first appeared, the psychologist asked, "What did you love best about your grandmother?"

"How she spent time with me. We went places and bought things."

"And are you afraid that other people in your family will die?"

"My mother," he finally admitted.

. . .

Obviously Jason's parents loved and cared about their little boy. Busy coping with their own grief, upset, and medico-legal details of the grandmother's dying, however, they had neglected to deal with the impact on a ten-year-old—and to connect this with his school phobia.

Definition

As the subject of more research papers in psychology journals than any other youthful emotion, school avoidance—refusal to attend school—is one of the most prevalent childhood fears. Although it occurs commonly at kindergarten age and again in third grade, it can be observed at various times, including adolescence. It occurs, in fact, wherever schools exist. The following words, which appeared in a 1984 issue of the British journal *Nursing Times,* were written by the manager of a community psychiatric nursing program in St. Albans, England:

> The problem of school non-attendees is a large one which can lead children and adolescents into the hands of many agencies and, for some, even into the courts and local authorities' care. The course these children tread can sometimes be long and traumatic, and some of the referrals were of children who had not been to school for months.

Symptoms

The symptoms begin with somatic complaints on school days, usually characterized by headaches or stomachaches. Anxiety about attending school is demonstrated by reluctance to leave the parent. Often the child makes the situation so difficult that the parent or parents must disrupt the work schedule to accommodate the child. Once in class, the child may visit the school nurse frequently.

1. Refusal to go to school;
2. Severe agitation at the time to leave for school;
3. Physical complaints about which the child is very serious, but which are not caused by illness.

Motivation

School avoidance can have numerous explanations. Generally, however, school phobics are neither truants nor poor students. One theory is that the child has anxiety about leaving home and separating from his mother. As in Jason's case, an event at home, such as a grandparent's death, parental illness or quarreling, or birth of a sibling, can trigger this fear. The child somehow gets the message that it is dangerous to leave parents at home.

Sometimes a real situation at school may frighten the child. In this case, a child may have been yelled at or punished by a teacher or hit by another child. When the youngster comes home and fusses over the incident, he receives so much attention that avoiding school seems a good idea.

What to Do

School avoidance is treated effectively in 98 percent of cases when treatment is initiated *promptly*. As with Jason, it consists of helping the child return to school while using techniques to lower anxiety. Some practitioners also recommend medication to alleviate the anxiety associated with separation. For successful, short-term use of drugs against panic and anxiety in severe cases of school refusal, see the next section of this chapter.

1. Speak with the child and attempt to get the facts about what may be going on at school. Know that although this problem tends to peak at about age eleven (the transition point from primary to secondary education), it can happen whenever the child is leaving the house daily or weekly to begin a new grade or school.

2. Look honestly at what feelings you and your spouse have about the child's leaving home. Sometimes, believe it or not, a parent doesn't want a child to leave. Although the motivation to have a child at home may make no intellectual sense, it can serve an important psychological need. A death in the family, an argument with a spouse that leaves one lonely, or simply missing a little person who has become a friend can cause a parent to regret a child's leaving.

These are all normal feelings!

The problem does not involve feeling this way; it emerges, rather, when a parent is not aware of such emotions and subtly encourages the child's staying home. Awareness is the key to determining what to do.

3. Let the child know that, although you understand his fears, there is no option but going to school. Try to picture what you would feel like if you were in the child's place, and then communicate this. Use sentences that say, "I know what you're feeling. I was afraid to go to school myself sometimes, but you have to go. It's a law. We don't really have a choice here. Let's go and see how we can make it easier for you. I know it's hard, but we have to do it."

If the child gets emotional and throws a tantrum, do not get upset or punish him. Telephone the school; wait until the next day; and accompany the child.

4. Let the school know what is happening. Education professionals often have an effective system to treat such situations.

5. Assuming you have the teacher's cooperation, take the child to school, even if for one hour while you wait with him.

Do this for two days; then extend the time to two hours, then half a day.

6. Praise and reward the child for such gradual successes.

7. If your child's reaction continues to be severe and does not respond to encouragement, consult your pediatrician. If your pediatrician recommends consulting a therapist, see the section on What to Do When Your Child Suffers a Phobic Fear, in Chapter 8.

USE OF MEDICATION FOR SCHOOL AVOIDANCE

One additional approach for treatment of school phobia is use of medication. Such a drug is *imipramine.* This has been tested thoroughly and appears to be effective. One of the tricyclic antidepressants, it was first found to alleviate panic attacks and severe separation anxiety in adult agoraphobics. Throughout the sixties, seventies, and eighties, usage of the drug has been tested and refined on those children whose primary symptom was also the inability to separate from those to whom they were closest, usually their mothers. Furthermore, it has succeeded in severe cases of bed-wetting and depression in children.

Without summarizing all these results, we quote from an interview of, and research paper by, Dr. Rachel Gittelman-Klein and Dr. Donald Klein of the New York Psychiatric Institute and College of Physicians and Surgeons, Columbia University, New York. (For exact references to the Gittelman-Klein work, see the Bibliography.)

In the Columbia program, school refusers who haven't responded to behavioral therapy and relaxation techniques first receive a thorough physical exam. Behavioral therapy is, of course, continued for the weeks while the child receives at least 75 milligrams per day of imipramine, depending on his weight (up to maximum of 200 milligrams per day). The child, who should be at least six years old, takes the medication by mouth each evening.

In good responders, no traces of separation anxiety remain. This is one of the few psychiatric treatments that, when successful, induces complete remission. . . .
Imipramine treatment need not be extended. Children usually respond completely within six to eight weeks. Medication should be continued for at least four weeks after remission, and then gradually withdrawn. . . . Only a minority of children have required continuous medication for six months or more. . . .

In good responders who can now leave home but still fear the school situation, "small doses of a benzodiazepine, such as 5 mg. of diazepam," are used as an adjunctive antianxiety agent but thus far have proved necessary only in some adolescents.

Side effects, especially dry mouth, are minor; rare children will also report sweating, tremor, constipation, or drowsiness.

Although about 70 percent to 90 percent of children either return to school after six weeks and/or report themselves "much improved," both researchers stress that imipramine is not a magic cure ("should not be viewed as a treatment that automatically leads to renewed school attendance"). Similar to clinical hypnosis, it modifies the child's level of anxiety in response to separation. That is, the stimuli—school and leaving home—remain, but the child no longer fears nor is so anxious about them. Using imipramine, many more also rid themselves of common symptoms secondary to school refusal, such as stomachaches, nausea, dizziness, and vague pains.

It is noteworthy, too, that of school refusers who receive a placebo drug, many fewer children (about 25 percent) manage to "return to school feeling better."

TEST ANXIETY

Philip, fifteen years old, was considered very bright by his teachers. One day in December, however, his parents were called to school because he was about to fail three of his five subjects—a humiliating handicap to a boy preparing for college.

At the meeting his teachers described his class performance as effective and informed. Although he also handled his homework correctly, the problem lay in his test performance. Because on tests he averaged but 25 out of 100 points, they had no choice but to fail him.

At school Philip had friends and worked well at academics —until he had to take a test. Then he would begin to perspire and feel dizzy, sometimes nearly fainting. In this state he could neither focus nor concentrate and remember. These real symptoms of test anxiety had worsened until they not only prevented him from functioning but were threatening the success of his whole schooling.

Philip's other and confounding problem was a common one: He did not feel he could discuss this situation with his parents. Indeed, the older he grew, the harder it became for him to talk with them, primarily because his mother seemed so eager for him to succeed that he dared not mention problems or conflicts along the way. When he began doing poorly and being embarrassed by it, therefore, he sought to hide the truth, especially from his parents.

Definition

This problem shows a syndrome characterized by symptoms of extreme anxiety, ranging from rapid pulse to full panic, when confronting the test situation.

Symptoms

1. Rapid heartbeat and breathing, dizziness, heightened G.S.R. (galvanic skin response), desire to urinate;
2. Inability to concentrate;
3. The feeling that previously learned information has vanished;
4. Urge to escape the examination room.

In its mildest form, at the beginning of test-taking the youngster will experience nervousness or butterflies in the stomach, which will subside as answering the questions proceeds. In more severe situations the child can recall none of the learned information and experiences full panic.

The net effect is that the child fails to show what he truly knows.

Motivation

Test anxiety, a serious problem that often goes unrecognized, strikes more often in adolescents than in younger children. The point of onset, which can occur at any time and creates an unbearable situation for the sufferer, relates chiefly to the child's growing fear of failure. The syndrome has nothing to do with intelligence or ability to study and prepare, even on unfavorite academic subjects.

Those prone to test anxiety are usually high achievers who pressure themselves to succeed. The evolution of this problem may go unnoticed until the child suddenly panics to discover he can't focus on test materials. While studying, he may have absorbed the information, including repeating and remembering it, yet in the pressured moment he draws an absolute blank after the test booklets or questions are passed around.

What to Do: Parent

1. If you notice a sudden change in a child's academic performance, especially in someone who functions well at school except for test-taking, examine whether the child may be experiencing test anxiety that may eventually undermine his whole scholastic record.

2. Talk with the child about whether a particular subject or teacher is somehow involved. Learn which situation or experience most upsets the child. Try to achieve this without placing extra pressure upon the child, since afflicted youngsters tend to be those already responding to parental demands or expectations to do well. Be sure not to ridicule or laugh at the child, or belittle his fear by saying, "All you have to do is try harder next time."

3. Talk with the teacher about alternative methods, such as an oral exam, to assess what your child knows about a particular subject. Work with the teacher to help him or her understand your child's emotions and problem.

4. Remove all possible pressure from the child by saying that you understand how difficult it is and don't want to upset him further. If the situation should persist, however, consult your pediatrician about obtaining help from a behavioral therapist who can retrain your child in how to face the exam situation. With a short treatment program, this condition should alleviate.

What to Do: Teacher

1. If you see that a student's work on a test does not represent what the child can do, try to understand what is occurring. Most teachers, however, are not trained to regard poor test performance as a coping difficulty that may afflict a child. Rather, they would consider it a lack of preparation or effort. The cues that differentiate test anxiety from poor preparation relate to a child's general attitude in class.

2. Realize that the child who suddenly starts failing tests or doing poorly may be suffering also (or even instead) from a secondary emotional reaction to some other home or school problem, causing him to react badly in other areas beyond tests. To determine exactly what is happening, try to talk with the youngster.

3. If the child, when questioned after class, gives excuses ("The dog ate my book"), the exam preparation likely has been inadequate. If, however, he says, "I don't understand what happens. I studied hard, but I just go blank," this can be a symptom of test anxiety.

4. Consult with the school psychologist or principal about how best to help the child, perhaps by temporary oral exams or relaxation exercises.

Remember: The most difficult part of this syndrome is that it doesn't look like fear. It simply resembles the behavior of the child who is unwilling to do assignments.

PERFORMANCE ANXIETY

Gineen, fifteen years old, was very bright. Although teachers found her quiet, she was a joy to teach and participated well in sports and extracurricular activities.

In English class, where she sat in the back of the room, she always paid attention, although never volunteering information. Because her teacher had just returned from an effective education workshop on techniques to encourage class participation, the teacher created student teams, eagerly appointing Gineen to lead one of them. Although all members would share preparing parts of the current assignment and report the information to Gineen, only she was supposed to report orally in front of all the other teams.

When her turn came, Gineen looked as if someone had exiled her to a leper colony. She just sat there, silent. She clearly couldn't respond. When one of the boys made a nasty comment, Gineen dropped her head onto her hands and began to sob. The teacher, having misread the signs of Gineen's problem, had also pushed her beyond the point the girl could tolerate.

Definition

Performance anxiety is characterized by a shy, quiet attitude and a terror of oral participation in class.

Symptoms

1. Fear, withdrawal, even panic when asked to perform publicly;
2. Occasional stammering, blushing, or sobbing when requested to answer questions.

Motivation

Performance anxiety is another of the subtle fears so difficult for the child. Like test anxiety, it is hard to differentiate from its lookalike—in this case and assuming equal effort at lesson preparation, the child who is merely shy, quiet, or normally nervous when called on.

This anxiety is frequently associated with peer group issues so important to the adolescent, such as fears about acceptance, fitting in, and never appearing different from one's friends. Its other cause can stem from trauma in the child who was, for example, teased by friends about an answer, ridiculed or insulted by a teacher, or humiliated during some public event, like a spelling bee or debate.

What to Do: Parent

1. If you learn that your child cannot speak in class, start by assuming there is no real need to worry, especially if the child can generally do the academic work. Remember the difference between shyness, which is embarrassing, and this disorder, which is truly painful. Although the child will sometimes talk with you about a difficult situation at school, he will usually avoid defining or describing the fears exactly and talk instead about how dreadful a particular subject or class experience is.

2. Try to discover precisely what about it is so disliked. Notice cues such as, "The teacher made me answer questions in front of everybody" or "The teacher made me talk in front of the other kids." Ask whether doing that is very hard, and try to learn more about the classroom experience. If you discover that a particular situation is terrifying the child, get help by following the steps in the Test Anxiety section in this chapter.

3. Surprisingly, the solution does not involve drilling the child in questions similar to those used by the teacher. This fear results from public performance, not poor study habits or preparation.

What to Do: Teacher

1. If you see a child who fits this definition, remember that forcing such a child to answer or perform will only worsen the situation. In fact, any heavy-handed approach can cause more severe reactions, such as trauma or refusal to return to school or a particular class.

2. Try to assess what the child's reticence means. Remember that with every action, the child makes a statement for the perceptive to notice. If he says, "I'm frightened of talking in front of others," respect that fear. Get some outside help by following the steps under Test Anxiety.

3. Try to take any immediate pressure off the child.

FEAR OF SUCCESS

Jeff, thirteen years old, had a history of school failure. Although he had been diagnosed early with a learning disability, his was not significant enough to warrant such poor scholastic performance. To compensate for poor grades, he often fought with the other boys.

At age eleven he changed schools and as a result had a fresh start. Things went very well for a while. His teachers liked him and he was getting B's and A's. As the year wore on, however, he stopped doing the work necessary to maintain his momentum. When his parents finally took him to a therapist, he was failing again. Through the therapy Jeff revealed that getting good grades put "too much pressure" on him. He was afraid he couldn't keep it up. As a result he took the path which was more familiar and more comfortable. Because he feared losing something if he succeeded, he refused to change and continued to fail.

Definition

This fear presents itself as a series of behaviors geared toward ensuring the child's failure, such as nonchalance about schoolwork and engaging in behavior which will result in failure. An added problem may be joining an undesirable peer group. Better-motivated students, especially girls, may also fail because they fear imagined aspects of success.

Symptoms

1. A child's regret and pain about self and the fact of failure;
2. A history of poor performance;
3. Stating "I don't care" as protection from guilt;
4. Avoiding necessary tasks, homework, and other assignments.

Motivation

Although fear of success is not a classic phobia, it is an area of intense recent interest for both academic and job performance in teenagers. Girls' fear of success, especially at nontraditional or difficult tasks or subjects like math and the sciences, has received much attention, and we have summarized some of this research below.

Like other anxieties in this section, fear of success relates to adolescent peer group pressures to conform, or at least not to distinguish oneself academically in a high school, where sports and popularity may matter more than grades to the average teenager. Hard work in any academic subject or field can be isolating, and success at one goal implies exclusion of other goals. Thus failure, although occasionally uncomfortable, can appear known and secure by comparison.

Those girls to whom popularity has become a major goal may have especially tempting reasons to perform poorly, since the average girl still does deal with conflicts, and even fear, about appearing smarter or more talented than the boys she dates. Added to this are various cultural expectations from parents and relatives about what a girl's goals "should" be— career or job, marriage and traditional career, marriage and nontraditional career.

Over the last decade *Sex Roles,* a social sciences journal, has carefully studied the consequences of the women's movement on topics affecting girls' lives, such as effect of maternal employment on daughters' goals, reactions of male employees to female supervisors, and aspects of girls' career motivation, including fear of success. Here are, for example, results of a study comparing teenage girls whose self-descriptions contained motive-to-avoid-success imagery with girls whose stories did not contain such imagery. Subjects who exhibited fear of success "reported lower expression of affection, lower self-concept with close associates, higher self-criticism, and higher external locus of control. In general, ambivalence characterized their view of themselves, their relationships with others, and their professional goals."

And what were these goals? The girls aspired to "traditional female occupations and were less concerned with making a major contribution to their field," compared with subjects not exhibiting such negative imagery. The latter "were more likely to choose atraditional female occupations, and their mothers were more likely to be employed in atraditional female occupations" (from a series of studies on nearly two hundred subjects by Rosemarie Anderson, "Motive to Avoid Success: A Profile," *Sex Roles* 4(2): 239–48, April 1978).

We include such results in this section because they show how confusing human motivation can be, unless you probe carefully. That is, you would expect that the girls aiming for nontraditional occupations would be the ones full of conflict and poor self-esteem ("Can I make it to dental school, and what will happen if I do?").

Dr. Matina Horner, president of Radcliffe College, has spent many years' research on motives to avoid career success in women. Some of her conclusions are that such women:

· Test abnormally high in anxiety;
· Are of demonstrably high intelligence;
· In the junior year of college, if not sooner, receive the second half of a parental double message—that now

a secure marriage matters more than entering or succeeding in the treacherous world of work, which is based in an always uncertain economic climate, etc.

. . .

To avoid dilemmas of both success and failure, a teenager, like other humans, is tempted to live only in the present, enjoying social life and preparing as little as possible for those dreaded situations, Responsibility and The Future.

What to Do: Parent

1. Understand the complex web of intrigue that fills an adolescent's life. Even the youngster who feels bad at not succeeding will rarely admit this. Do your best to ascertain the truth as delicately as possible. For example, don't yell at the child about poor grades. Sometimes professional help can guide the child toward improved study habits.

2. Try to help the child experience success without making this a requisite for acceptance. Set up a system of study for the child that helps him organize his work. Sometimes teachers can provide a homework sheet listing assignments so you can check these with him.

3. Find some way to reward successes without providing much secondary attention to failures. If the child gets a better grade during one marking period, make sure that you notice and compliment this.

4. Seek the school's help so that both teacher and principal will learn of your concern and efforts to affect the situation. Address the issue of this fear. Try not to sound like an "overly concerned parent," but help them understand the issue.

5. Examine your own motives, including any mixed or double messages you may be transmitting. In order to feel needed or wanted, some parents unwittingly encourage a child's failure by such statements as, "Math was always too hard for you. Try something easier," "Nobody in our family ever tried that. How could you hope to make it?", or "Girls are no good at that." These statements, which contain generalizing words like "nobody," "everybody," "always," "never," overtly or subtly discourage the young person, who may then start repeating them about his own chances.

Two excellent books to help examine the "message behind the message" are *Nobody's Perfect, How to Give Criticism and Get Results* by Dr. Hendrie Weisinger and Norman M. Lobsenz (Stratford Press, Los Angeles, 1981; distributed by Harper & Row) and *The Gentle Art of Verbal Self-Defense* by Suzette Haden Elgin (Dorset Press/Prentice Hall, Englewood Cliffs, New Jersey, 1980).

What to Do: Teacher

1. Try to understand the statements behind a teen's failing behavior.

2. Avoid further confrontations over grades or classroom conduct.

3. Try to devise ways to make small successes possible for the child, and reward these without embarrassing him in front of the peer group.

4. Seek help from the school administration.

CHAPTER 8

. . .

Storms in the Dark: Nature-related Phobias

INTRODUCTION: THE NATURE OF PHOBIA

I won't walk anywhere near trees—even a photograph of a caterpillar makes me panicky. Once, when I was young, a small caterpillar fell out of a tree onto my head. I started tearing at my hair and screaming: "Oh, my God! Get it off me! Get it off me!" . . . My father must have heard me because he ran over and tried to calm me down. I kept screaming and he kept saying, "It's only a bug!" Then he slapped me. I don't think I ever forgave him for that. (Diane V.)

I was around five years old. I was playing on the lawn of a neighbor about six houses from my house. When I decided to leave, I looked around for the direction of my home. But all I could see on both sides were more big lawns going endlessly in a long row. . . . Panic set in, and I became so gripped with fear that my legs fell from under me. Then I lost my voice and couldn't scream for help. I felt as if I was in a terrible nightmare and couldn't wake up. (Vicky J.; both patients quoted from Dr. Harold N. Levinson's and Steven Carter's *Phobia Free*)

No one reading these first-person anecdotes can deny the force of the terror behind the words—nor the unfortunate response of the father who, losing patience with the irrational, probably reinforced its power over his daughter.

Nature-related terrors (of insects, animals, storms, the dark, and so forth) are especially tragic because various studies show them as the one major fear group—compared with social, personal, sexual, or political—that normally *decreases* as children mature.

As stated at the beginning of this book, the one thousand scientifically acknowledged phobias affect about 10 percent of this country's population. Many—blessedly—remain as rare as the objects, such as sharks, that evoke them. Others, like agoraphobia, the onset of which you see above in Vicky J.'s story, are distressingly common; of 25 million U.S. residents with incapacitating terrors, 12 million are agoraphobics (fear open spaces). And of these, at least three fourths are women.

According to psychiatrist Isaac M. Marks, ". . . women constitute 75% of the agoraphobic population, 95% of the animal phobic population, 60% of social phobics" (quoted in Robert DuPont's *Phobia: A Comprehensive Summary of Modern Treatments*). In some agoraphobic studies, women form more than 90 percent of subjects. Since women also exceed men in anxiety-related disorders, psychiatric problems, insomnia, and suicide attempts, many have wondered whether traditional expectations of women as dependent, fearful, submissive, and emotional are responsible for these alarming numbers. Whatever the reasons, it is obvious that many of these women were not helped in childhood to conquer their terrors.

The study of phobias is ancient. Two thousand years ago the "father of medicine," Hippocrates, described a man who could not walk near a precipice or even a ditch and was "beset by terror" upon hearing the notes of a flute played at night, even during busy banquets. He seems to have suffered from a fear of heights and displaced fears of both flute music and the dark. During the day he could hear a flute "without feeling any emotion."

If you have read the preceding chapter on school-related phobias, you probably noted the following qualities that we summarize here, since they form the guidelines on how to differentiate a fear from a phobia. A phobia is characterized by:

- A pattern of avoidance of the dreaded situation;
- An intensity of symptoms and behavior to the point of deranging ordinary life and functions;
- A fear of the panic attack itself and feelings caused by the phobia (the victim begins to fear the fear);
- A significant distress, including extreme self-consciousness, from knowing the emotions to be excessive and unreasonable;
- Perceptual distortions of various kinds;
- Despair about a solution to any of these problems;
- For simple or specific phobias, the ability to function adequately away from the phobic object;
- A condition independent of any other mental disorder, such as schizophrenia or an obsessive-compulsive problem;
- Possible lag time between fearsome exposure and appearance of the phobia;
- Possible generalizing of the phobia to other objects or related situations.

Although the variety of situations about which people, including children, can become phobic is legion, the thoughts that afflict them are blessedly few and predictably linked to other "survival emotions" (love, anger, loneliness):

1. Fear of dying, including fear of helplessness or solitude;

2. Fear of being lost;
3. Fear of losing control (fainting, cursing, becoming violent);
4. Fear of being ridiculous, shaming or embarrassing oneself.

For further information and a summary of theories on origins of phobias or for advice on helping a youngster whose symptoms are verging into phobia, see the Afterword.

Finally, here are further characteristics of phobic people that demonstrate what a burden they carry. Such individuals are apt to be:

- Hyperreactive;
- Overimaginative, plagued with "What if?" worries about the future;
- Perfectionistic, with immense desire to do tasks correctly and please others;
- Friendly, conscientious, sensitive as students, employees, spouses;
- Exaggeratedly aware of others' reactions to them.

Regarding the idea of hypersensitivity (it's not what happens to us; it's what we make of it), John Steinbeck in *East of Eden* summarized a phobic sequence of emotions and the panoply of possible responses:

The greatest terror a child can have is that he is not loved, and rejection is the hell he fears . . . and with rejection comes anger, and with anger, some kind of crime in revenge. . . . One child, refused the love he craves, kicks the cat and hides his secret guilt; another steals so that money will make him loved; and the third conquers the world.

WHAT TO DO WHEN YOUR CHILD SUFFERS A PHOBIC FEAR

1. Contact your pediatrician. Your doctor has been trained to spot psychological problems and through his experience can either offer advice or refer you to the proper source for help.

Should you feel neither listened to nor taken seriously, however, and are still concerned, ask sooner, rather than later, for a referral. For example, children do "grow out of" many fears, but none of the phobias are likely to be in this easier group.

2. When contacting the agency or person recommended, be an informed consumer. Unfortunately, not all people in the helping professions are equal—nor does their expertise depend on the lavishness of their office or the number of degrees on its wall. If necessary, shop around for a therapist. Your pediatrician or other doctor should not be offended if you interview two or three practitioners to learn their methods and views on phobias and related problems.

3. Speak to the person who will actually help your child. Does he make sense? Explain procedures clearly? Have a treatment plan and an estimate of its length and cost?

As you have probably noted with other medical personnel, finding competent, pleasant help is not unlike finding a pair of shoes that fit properly. The same last may fit different feet differently, and it matters that you attain a good fit.

·   ·   ·

To summarize, here are some wise, if tragic, words by Dr. John T. Wood (himself a recovered phobic) in his book *What Are You Afraid Of?*:

Along this path of fear we are traveling, phobias are the Stop signs. They are the "Do Not Enter—Wrong Way" warnings we see on the freeway ramps. They are the signals, based on some reality in the past and, in most cases, long since useless, that tell us not to proceed.

Learning how to help your child "proceed" is the purpose of this book, as you set about defining your child's problem and assessing its severity.

PHOBIA OF THE DARK

Jennifer was twelve when her mother was involved in an auto accident one rainy night. She had just turned off her light before sleep when the phone rang downstairs. After she heard her father running, she sensed the uneasy commotion that accompanies something terrible. She was half out of bed in the dark when her father bolted into her room. "Mommy's hurt!" he exclaimed. "Get dressed. We have to go."

Jennifer was scared. In the blackness she couldn't see, yet she knew something dreadful had happened.

Having groped for the light, she quickly dressed while the words, "Mommy's hurt! Mommy's hurt!" vibrated through her mind. Her head spun, and she couldn't catch her breath.

Her father sped the car over the damp streets toward the hospital. When they finally arrived at the right room, she couldn't recognize her mother. Tubes, bandages, and splints bristled from every part of the woman's body.

Terrified, Jennifer began to wail long, animal-like cries.

Several weeks later she began to feel severe anxiety whenever the lights were turned off at bedtime. Next she needed the light on while she slept. Shortly after this, she avoided any darkened rooms or buildings.

Jennifer's mother recovered after a month in the hospital and two months in a nursing home.

Definition

Phobia of the dark occurs when the afflicted person avoids dark places with such intensity that ordinary life, including bedtime or travel, can become impossible.

Motivation

Jennifer's state vividly demonstrates the power of *displacement*. That is, the emotions (terror and uncertainty over her mother's condition) that might have led another person to dread driving or rain as the source of the fearsome incident produced in Jennifer an almost accidental, but wholly real, reaction to one dark room that then generalized to all dark places. Such incidents can range from the upset of seeing a horror movie just before bed, through Jennifer's unintentional, even coincidental, coupling of events (dark + accident), to—ultimately—the trauma produced by an angry parent who intentionally locks a child in a dark closet. The result is a youngster who carries the average child's fear of the dark to dramatic lengths.

In psychoanalytic (Freudian) theory of phobia formation, the phobia binds and then displaces free-floating anxiety about some object, person, or situation onto another object that can ordinarily be avoided, such as horses, snakes, or sharks. Freud's classic description of a phobia of horses in a five-year-old boy, Little Hans, revealed a picture of a child who loved his mother and feared imagined retaliation from his father. Having seen a horse fall in a park, he displaced his own aggressive wishes against his father onto this animal, which generalized to a fear of all horses, which he could then avoid and thus manage his anxiety.

For further information on such theories and their operation within the mind as it confronts reality, see the Afterword.

What to Do

1. Pay attention to the child's distress, and resist the urge to ridicule or belittle even if the phobic object seems unusual or ridiculous for a child of a certain age.

2. Try to ascertain what the child truly fears—what trauma may have become associated with an object or situation related or seemingly unrelated.

3. Know that the difference between a fear and a phobia of the dark is that the latter is not only intense but unremitting.

4. If the condition persists, contact your pediatrician for help and referral.

PHOBIA OF ANIMALS

Kim, a six-year-old girl, lived in a large town in northern Connecticut. Suddenly, one day in August, she refused to approach any of the neighborhood cats or dogs if she saw one on the street. Next she peered nervously from the living room window, refusing to go outdoors if any dog was playing with the local children. By the end of a week she had become reluctant to leave the house at all.

Kim's mother, who grew increasingly concerned about her behavior, also began to dread outings because the girl became hysterical whenever it was time to leave.

Two weeks before the entire sequence began, the parents of a friend, Jean, had taken both girls to see *Cujo* at the local drive-in theater. This is a frightening movie starring an immense and rabid St. Bernard dog. This animal was terrifying from the beginning of the film. Yet later that night, both girls had fallen asleep, and Kim spent the rest of the night at her friend's house without a problem.

Next morning, however, as the girls played with Jean's cocker spaniel, the dog, which had tired of getting his ears pulled, snapped at Kim. He then lunged and nipped her on the arm. As Jean's mother washed the bite, she scolded, "You know Scrubby's old now. Why did you tease him?" Both girls looked ashamed and then returned to their play.

When Kim arrived home, she told her mother about the overnight visit, and all seemed well until Kim went outdoors and saw a neighbor walking his black dog with the floppy ears.

With school about to begin in a week and Kim unable to get beyond the front door, her mother desperately phoned the family doctor for help.

Motivation

Phobia of a particular animal can begin anytime during childhood, depending on circumstances. Most animal phobias that become or remain incapacitating commence before the age of eight, and the choice of animals or insects is surprisingly limited (see Fear of Animals sections in earlier chapters), usually involving common domesticated animals (horses, cats, dogs), reptiles, or insects. That is, fear of tigers or dinosaurs is outgrown once the child realizes how rare or even extinct many wild creatures have become.

As with most phobias termed "simple" or "specific" (limited to one situation or object), an animal phobia usually results from a serendipitous pairing of exposure to an animal with some incident that becomes associated with it, such as the combination of an actual bite with the chime of a bell or of an animal injury to a parent with the child present. At other times, a near-encounter with a universally disliked beast, such as a snake or worm, coupled with a child's vivid imagination, is sufficient to precipitate a problem. Very often there is a delay between the incident and the reaction.

Whatever has occurred, the child's emotions and mind have registered it as trauma and begun to respond accordingly.

What to Do

1. Assess the impact of the phobia on the life of the child or adolescent and your family. If it does not cause major disruption, then you probably need not seek special help or treatment. These fears will often pass without complication.

2. If, however, the phobia has begun to generalize, disrupt normal life, or produce undue discomfort, follow the procedure described earlier in this chapter and contact your pediatrician.

PHOBIA OF STORMS (AUDITORY)

Rita was twelve when the phobic reaction first occurred. Because she disliked having it, she ran to her mother for help. At first she'd felt nervous and then panicky whenever the sky lowered and thunder began. Becoming dizzy, she couldn't catch her breath. As the perspiration began, she felt all hot and cold. Finally she couldn't stand it.

It had begun one day about six weeks earlier, while she walked home from school. The clouds, which had massed all day, now reached that mauve gray that portends a thunderstorm. As she rushed to beat the storm, she found herself caught in it. A few blocks from school, the sky burst open; thunder cracked, and lightning shattered the air. The downpour then forced her into a doorway.

As she stood, soaked and panting, a man ducked into the same doorway and bumped her against the wall. Tall and wearing a smelly shirt, he was unshaven and seemed to fill the whole space. "Sorry," he said as he steadied her elbow. "Hi, little girl," he added. "Sure is raining, huh?" As he gazed up and down her soaked hair and dress, Rita suddenly became very frightened. She didn't know why—only that she must escape from this creepy man.

Bursting out into the rain, she dashed all the way home, not daring to look back.

Several weeks later the phobia emerged. Whenever a storm threatened or the sky clouded suddenly, she couldn't force herself beyond the front porch. When her father yelled at her, she was too upset and ashamed to tell anyone what had happened.

Motivation

Phobias involving storms can result from any negative experience that occurs simultaneously with the noise and danger of lightning, downpour, winds, or blizzard. During the storm the child will cower or seek out the parents for security and comfort. The phobia can result either from actual trauma (injury) during a storm or from (as here) some storm-related event.

What to Do

1. Although it is hard for anyone who hasn't experienced a phobic episode to understand how paralyzing it is, do not belittle your child for what may seem an excessive reaction to a natural event.

2. If the child will talk about what has occurred, analyze the experience.

3. Seek help promptly for any child who demonstrates extreme agitation.

WATER PHOBIA

Eight-year-old Ginny was spending a summer day at the beach with her parents. She was the older of two sisters, and outings were significant to the entire family. A bright and energetic child, she sometimes enthusiastically overdid her activities.

As she and her father were walking the shoreline, large blue waves crashed and sucked at their feet. Ginny suddenly decided it would be fun to rush one or two of them. Luckily her father was watching, because Ginny rushed forward just as a giant wave swelled. Taking her by surprise, in an instant it had tumbled her upside down under the surge of water.

As lifeguards blew whistles, Ginny's father jumped in to grab the small body before the undertow sucked her away.

Coughing and shaken, Ginny followed her father back to the rest of her family. Her mother, whose face had gone white, wrapped the trembling, now-sobbing girl into a towel.

Three weeks later, during the next beach outing, Ginny insisted the blanket be put high on the sand, fifty feet from the water. Furthermore, she fretted constantly about whether the tide was truly going in or out.

Next she refused to approach the lake at her grandparents' house in the country. Although she could look at a body of water from a car window, she could no longer tolerate walking near one.

Motivation

This is not a classic phobia so much as a basic survival fear that usually occurs in response to trauma involving a life-threatening incident. What occurs in one situation can generalize, however, as in Ginny's story until even a youngster who knows how to swim is left helpless in places that present no immediate danger (a quiet country lake).

What to Do

1. Help the child experience the feared situation again—cautiously. Do not force or push the child into the water.

Emphasize all the safety measures you are taking—holding hands, giving the child a flotation vest, checking that the tide is out, and so forth.

2. Try to get the child back into some body of water with an adult as soon as possible.

3. If the fear persists and begins to generalize, consult professional help, since this fear is easily remedied with proper intervention.

CHAPTER 9

. . .

Nettled by Needles:
Health-related Phobias

INTRODUCTION

Many psychologists have connected health fears and phobias to one of humankind's original instincts—the fight for self-preservation and the terror of pain and dying. Although intellectually everyone "knows," for instance, that treatment in the hospital or a dentist's chair occasionally become necessary, the primitive mind residing in all of us begins to scream, "Why me? Why now? Let me out of here."

And every new case of phobia records both the fight and the flight.

PHOBIA OF PERSONAL INJURY

Fifteen-year-old John was always shy and quiet. His school, a good one, offered an active sports program that John usually avoided. Since he took alternate courses to meet his physical education requirement, no one noticed his absence from competitive games and contact sports.

His unwitting parents became the ones who pushed him to try himself at soccer. "It'll look good on your college record," they insisted. "Just try out for the team. If they don't accept you, you don't have to do it."

Although John complained and found excuses to miss the first tryout session, his mother threatened that if he missed the second one, he'd lose his allowance and other privileges at home.

A half hour before the tryout, John couldn't stand the conflict anymore. In the kitchen he threw a fit of such proportions —flinging and smashing pots, dishes, and stools while he yelled that he hated school and home both—that he terrified his mother. She rapidly sought professional help.

At the evaluation, John spoke freely about his fear of getting hurt, breaking something, or losing an eye and how he could not even stand to watch any of the ball sports on television. Nor did he understand how his parents could force him to do something he so hated.

Motivation

Phobias about injury occur more frequently than we think. Because the symptoms are disguised by or as lack of interest, dislike, or ridicule of sports, many children thus avoid the feared situation without revealing how afraid they are of physical injury, major or minor.

The source of the fear may lie in reactions to events or games that have been painful. A further explanation can involve overprotective parents who warn youngsters, especially girls, of dangers both real and imaginary, should they dare to enter the rough and tumble of neighborhood or playground activity.

What to Do

1. Since a major hurdle with this phobia is to uncover its existence, analyze your child's previous attitude toward sports, gym classes, or physical activities. Has it suddenly or gradually changed?

2. If your child is a teenager, try to distinguish the phobia from the adolescent's ordinary worries over body image or physical clumsiness that may also be making him reluctant to exhibit and perform on the athletic field or gym floor.

3. Try to encourage the child to discuss the fear.

4. Assess whether the fear is reasonable—how dangerous the sport truly is. Fearing football is, in fact, sensible; fearing tennis or badminton probably isn't.

5. Contact the school, searching for a sympathetic guidance counselor or gym teacher. Try to switch your child to a less-threatening sport or noncompetitive activity to fulfill the physical education requirement. Beware and avoid the heavy-handed "no sissies here" approach.

6. If the child has a real disability, such as poor vision or other physical problems, tell the truth about this if the school officials do not already know.

7. If the phobia persists and begins to generalize to other physical activities, seek professional help.

PHOBIA OF HOSPITALS

Fourteen-year-old Gerald was a healthy normal boy who enjoyed a close relationship with both parents. His father worked for a construction company that installed windows and doors in large buildings. During Gerald's ninth-grade year, his father fell from a fourth-story window onto a patch of grass in front of an apartment building. Although an awning had partly broken his fall, he lay unconscious and bleeding.

When Gerald returned from school, he found his mother's note saying that she had rushed to the hospital to stay with his father. Gerald followed. After finding his father's room, he saw a horrifying vision—his father covered with bandages while he panted into a tube stuck down his throat. Indeed, tubes, wires, and machines protruded everywhere. Dumbstruck, Gerald stood beside his mother, who had become a sobbing, hysterical wreck. The whole room reeked so strongly of alcohol and chemicals that the boy could hardly breathe. Nor could he understand how anybody could recover in a place like this. At the bedside, silent nurses came and did mysterious maintenance around the machinery.

Gerald's father died a few hours later. His uncle had to arrive and organize the funeral because his mother could not stop crying. For three days Gerald skipped school, sat in his room listening to music, and cried too. The impact on all their lives was evident.

When Gerald developed a phobia of hospitals shortly afterward, he couldn't pass the hospital where his father had died without developing an acute anxiety attack. During the first attack he shook so badly that people who tried to help assumed he was taking drugs. He soon avoided the whole end of North Street where the hospital stood.

Motivation

This phobia is clearly and unfortunately associated with trauma that has occurred inside a hospital. Although Gerald's father died suddenly, giving the family no time to adjust to the thought or fact of death, such a phobia can also result from witnessing a lingering death filled with similar medical apparatus and technology. Any trauma associated with a hospital can result in this phobia.

What to Do

1. Seek professional help for the child as soon as possible.

2. In the case of the child being hospitalized, seek a friendly nurse or a medical social worker within the hospital who will take time to answer the family's questions on medical or hospital procedure. Include the child in part or all of this talk. Such a social worker will also help arrange a meeting with your doctor if the crisis has not allowed time for this. This solution is not always possible, however.

3. When the first emergency has passed, help the child go by or even reenter the feared building. Be sure to show that you do not fear the building too.

PHOBIA OF NEEDLES

Martina, a healthy fourteen-year-old, was successful in school and had made good friends. In fact, she was happy most of the time—until she developed a fear of injections.

Because she had been sick for several weeks with something that resembled mononucleosis, her pediatrician requested blood samples to analyze the cause of her illness. The technician, who was joking around with a coworker, missed her vein the first time and had to repeat the needle insertion. Although this experience was not pleasant, Martina seemed to endure it well.

The doctor decided she was suffering from a particular virus that was making the rounds that winter. After a further week of sickness that included a high fever, Martina felt well enough to return to school.

Two months later a new problem began at the dentist's office. During a routine visit a cavity was discovered that would require drilling. As the dentist prepared the novocaine injection, Martina took one look at it and became hysterical. She continued to be so agitated that her mother had to drive her home. She also refused to go back.

No wrath or determination exceeds that of a fourteen-year-old who has made up her mind. She fought with her parents; she screamed and shouted that she would not have anything to do with that dentist.

Her parents were both mystified and concerned. What could have happened in the dentist's chair?

Then Martina calmed enough to admit she was petrified of the novocaine injection required to drill a tooth. Finally she needed general anesthesia to get her annual dental work done at all.

Motivation

This phobia, which is, interestingly, more common in girls than boys, usually results from an unpleasant previous experience involving needles. Prompt help is needed to prevent the fear from becoming a phobia and to ensure that it doesn't generalize from the dentist to every hospital or doctor visit requiring blood samples or injections. If the child is hospitalized, adding illness and separation anxiety to an existing terror of needles, the situation can become totally unmanageable.

A helpful article is "The Fear of Needles in Children" (David Fassler, M.D., *American Journal of Orthopsychiatry* 55[3]: 371–77, 1985). It describes work with thirty-nine children, aged three through nine, who were divided into two groups, both needing injections. Only 10 percent of the group that received "empathetic support" cried in anticipation of the needle, while nearly 53 percent of those who received only directive, impersonal support cried.

The empathetically supported children heard the lab technician say the following:

> I'm not doing this because you did anything wrong, but just to help you get well. . . . In a minute, I'm going to stick you. You're probably feeling a little scared and it's

going to hurt a little bit, but it won't last long. And I don't mind if you cry because that's only natural.

Although this doesn't seem to us a stunning example of empathy, apparently it was unexpected and welcome enough in that antiseptic setting to keep 90 percent of the children from crying.

By contrast, the children who received only "directive preparation" were told, "In a minute I'm going to stick you. I want you to stay still and not move because if you jerk your arm or flex, I may have to stick you again." Faced with such a threat, more than half of them cried from anticipated pain.

One pediatrician we know uses a distraction technique. She says to the child, "When you count to three, the injection will be all over. Now look at me and begin counting, One . . . two . . . three." Although the child expects the needle at the end of three, the doctor gives it quickly at two while the patient is distracted by counting and watching her face. She says some children feel nothing and wind up asking "When are you going to give me the shot?", at which point she happily informs them it's all over.

What to Do

1. Try to assess what the child truly fears about the doctor or dentist visit.
2. If it is the needle, don't ridicule the fear or force the child into the office or lab.
3. Do not let your own possible fear of needles intrude here. For a younger child, bring a toy or game to distract him until the injection is finished.
4. Ask whether injections usually given in the buttocks can as easily be given in the arm (where they usually hurt less during and afterward), and make sure you or the child remembers to vary the arms.

5. Don't deceive the child about the duration or intensity of the experience. Ask the dentist or other personnel not to use euphemisms like "This won't hurt a bit," which naturally makes the child say or think "Of course, because it's not hurting *you.*"

6. Stay with the child, holding his hand or rubbing his back to comfort him and indicate that you are not yourself nervous or upset.

CHAPTER 10

. . .

Far from the Crowd: Interpersonal Phobias

PHOBIA OF SOCIAL CONTACT (EXCESSIVE SHYNESS)

Kevin was a nine-year-old boy who had experienced much difficulty, both physical and social, in his short life. As an only child of older parents, he was always treated as "special," yet he certainly had not become spoiled because of this. Indeed, his intense lack of self-confidence rendered him quite the opposite.

As an infant, he had required several operations to correct a congenital problem with his knees. He had also needed surgery to correct the muscles that had made his eyes cross. Both unfortunate problems had, of course, exposed him to much merciless teasing by other children.

Kevin had no close friends, nor had he ever developed effective peer relationships. At school he stayed to himself; at home he rarely ventured outdoors. He could not compete in games. When forced into a situation that demanded participation, such as choosing sides for a school team, he became anxious and withdrew to a corner where the other children, who called him "sissy" and "baby," gladly let him stay.

By the fourth grade his apparent "shyness" had become a phobia of social contact.

Motivation

It is crucial to distinguish social contact phobia from varying degrees of shyness, which is a personality trait rather than a developmental phenomenon. That is, some people are simply more introverted than others. Some children have quiet or shy parents who themselves lack social skills, and many children are normally shy in new or unfamiliar situations, like the first day of school or camp or visiting a strange house. Some shyness stems from environment. For instance, in a large city, if children cannot by themselves leave the floor of their apartment building—let alone the building or street itself—they may lack the frequent, easy social contact that produces social grace.

When such normal shyness has developed into total lack of self-esteem and confidence in one's abilities or appearance, the child needs help.

What to Do

1. Try to analyze when or where your child seems excessively shy or greatly anxious about social contact. Try to determine whether something particular and traumatic occurred in one situation or whether the child shrinks from meeting all people.

2. At times children with this disorder will improve spontaneously or readily after, for example, help from a sympathetic teacher or camp counselor. If the child's functioning is disrupted and if, after two months, the child remains awed or anxious in social situations, secure professional help.

ELECTIVE MUTISM

Twelve of the 15 children were not only silent, but also shy and reticent. If asked to sit, stand, or walk, they would comply—but woodenly. They would not paint, play, or eat. . . . Although aware of their surroundings, the EM youngsters apparently preferred to be left alone or with another child who was a relative (and, in some cases, also electively mute). While with strangers, their facial expression and slow and rigid body movements did not change even if their mother or siblings were present. (M. Lesser-Katz, "Stranger Reaction and Elective Mutism in Young Children," *American Journal of Orthopsychiatry* 56[3]:458–69, 7/86)

Definition

Elective mutism is a continuous refusal to speak in almost all social situations, including school, despite ability to comprehend spoken language and to speak. These children may communicate by gestures, by nodding or shaking the head or, in some cases, by monosyllables or short, monotone utterances. Afflicted children generally have normal language skills, although some show delayed language development. Their refusal to speak is not due to language insufficiency or another mental disorder.

Symptoms

1. Refusal to use normal language abilities ("She can speak, but she won't");
2. Onset before the age of five, more frequently in girls than in boys;
3. Clinging, excessive shyness, or freezing in the dreaded situation;

4. School refusal that may lead to school failure;
5. Tantrums and other oppositional behavior before or during the dreaded situation.

Motivation

Elective mutism—with its associated features of shyness, stranger anxiety, or social withdrawal—creates a disturbance that severely impairs functioning. It can also be but one symptom of many psychiatric, learning, or behavioral disorders that afflict children.

In its simpler form, it can result from overprotective parents who themselves lack social or English-language skills. The above group of children, for instance, came from a Spanish-speaking neighborhood in Chicago "where people tend to keep to themselves and to regard the environment outside their homes as hostile, or at least unfriendly. . . . Since most depend on public assistance, it is also important for them to keep other sources of income from becoming widely known."

Elective mutism may result from trauma or various environmental changes, such as death of a loved one or being forced within a school situation. Since the disorder often results from reaction to such environmental change (new caretaker, school, or language), it is not, therefore, a classic phobia (a fear either innate or based in the child's own normal development).

As with many conditions, there can be secondary gains for the child. These include achieving power through creating family anxiety; enjoyment of omnipotent fantasies; and expression of hostility by the child who uses silence as a weapon.

What to Do

1. Begin by trying to differentiate elective mutism from normal shyness, stranger anxiety, and fear of new situations. It

is also crucial to differentiate between a child who *chooses* to be mute and one who falls silent from trauma or stress in a particular locale.

2. If the mutism continues, begin with a physical exam by your child's pediatrician and follow the doctor's advice for further professional help. Seek help quickly, since this disorder, like school phobia, responds well to behavioral therapy in the otherwise normal child.

A full evaluation at a speech and hearing clinic of a teaching hospital or by a private therapist who specializes in such assessment is usually needed, both for otherwise normal children and those suspected of suffering from speech pathologies or mental retardation.

3. Know that parents and other caretakers play a vital role in successful recovery of the child's speech. Sue, a friend of ours in California, sought help for one of her sons, Jimmy, because he would hardly speak at all, having remained silent for the first two weeks of kindergarten. She and her husband received the following advice, which they used while continuing the boy's therapy sessions:

> We were taught to hold him firmly on our laps or hold his head and let him loose only if he talked. That made silence expensive for him, because much as he disliked talking, he disliked being held even more. So he finally opened up and said, "I want to get down." Granting his wish, we would praise him enthusiastically for talking.
>
> We also became very "stupid" at reading his body language. Instead of figuring out what he wanted, we asked him to tell us in words. At last he did. . . .

Besides elective mutism, Jimmy experienced numerous learning disabilities during the early years of school. However, adds Sue with her characteristic wit:

After our son was pushed into using language, he discovered it was useful and fun. At four, he spoke rarely. At six, he spoke a little more. At eight, he got acquainted with new neighbors who refused to believe he was ever mute. As a young adult, he can talk you under the table.

AGORAPHOBIA

"The claustrophobic, he wants to get near a window: I want to be near a door." (Statement by an agoraphobic woman)

Definition

Agoraphobia is a fear of being trapped and having a panic attack in a public place (to differentiate it from the enclosed spaces that the claustrophobe fears).

Such an incident may occur on a train or in a ballpark or some other crowded area from which escape is difficult. When the victim avoids being placed in such a situation, the phobia thus begins. This classic phobia can generalize until the victim is unable to leave the house at all.

Symptoms

1. Marked fear of being alone in public places or anywhere from which escape or flight is impeded, such as a crowded department store, beach, heavy traffic, bridge, or tunnel;
2. Panic attacks, involving dizziness, nausea, shortness of breath, "jelly legs," inability to move;
3. Anticipatory fear of such attacks until the sufferer has become "phobophobic" (afraid of the fear itself);
4. Restriction upon normal activities, insistence upon being accompanied to appointments, shopping, and so forth;

5. Onset in late adolescence or early twenties, commonly in women.

Motivation

Although agorapobia usually begins beyond age sixteen, we include it in this book for two reasons. First, it is often preceded by an avoidance disorder involving death of a loved one or separation anxiety in some form, such as school phobia. Secondly, it has become by far the leading phobia problem in the United States (estimated 12 million of 25 million phobics).

One adult agoraphobic, Vicky J. (discussed at the beginning of Chapter 8), traced the start of her problem to the panic attack she experienced at age five upon realizing how far she had strayed from her own home within the vast tract of open lawns and suburban houses. Her terror, paralysis, and voice loss ended only after she had spotted someone who looked like her sister and she had crawled on her elbows (since her legs no longer worked) across several neighbors' lawns. Her attempt at flight from the situation resembled what happens to someone who has suffered a cerebral hemorrhage and then tries to move or speak.

What to Do

1. Examine what has happened to your child or teenager, especially possible trauma involving a public place.

2. Seek professional help promptly before this phobia worsens or generalizes.

CHAPTER 11

· · ·

Further Hints:
What to Do If—

As you read parts or all of the preceding chapters, did your thoughts resemble any of the following:

- "Well, that's a good idea, but my husband (or wife) would never agree."
- "My kid is so stubborn, and his symptoms aren't described exactly. What can I do?"
- "My daughter's very bright. She sees right through anything simplistic."
- "My son now exaggerates his fear because he likes all the attention it's getting him."

This chapter contains answers to these and other realistic dilemmas that confront the parent who tries to apply a rule or advice, however generally valid, to a confusingly specific situation.

For any of these situations, it also helps to read the beginning of Chapter 8 on how to differentiate a fear from a phobia.

SPOUSES' DISAGREEMENT

For many reasons a couple may disagree on whether a child's problem exists and, if so, on its nature and potential solution. Indeed, it is probably wishful thinking to imagine that two parents will share the same intuition or perception about a development, whether good or difficult, in one of their own children. One parent may prefer discipline, whereas the other —perhaps in compensation—may overprotect. If one parent denies the child's symptoms, further refusing even to listen to a worried partner, arguments and blaming about the source and solution of the problem then easily erupt.

In the case of a phobic child who absolutely refuses to swim, cross a yard, or pet a dog, an underreactive parent will commonly deny or excuse, terming the child "shy" or "quiet" instead of "terrified." And the parent who denies may also become the one who ridicules or pushes the child into the water or the path of the feared object.

At the other extreme, an overreactive parent excuses in the opposite direction, babying the child to the point of arousing jealousy and anger in other family members not so favored.

Moreover, parents, whether under- or over-reactive, may use the child's problem or, conversely, deny one exists to score points against partners who, they believe, are not cooperating or understanding in other areas of family life. It is tempting to advocate a child's "rights" or viewpoint after one has despaired of communicating one's own during clashes over something prior to the child's fear. If a wife, for instance, fears her husband won't listen to her recounting one of her own problems, then she may use the child's dilemma to bore into his psyche or at least swivel it momentarily away from the TV.

What to Do

1. Start by listening to each other's opinions on the nature or severity of the child's problem. When one person has finished speaking, the other should repeat and summarize as fairly as possible what has just been said. "Then you feel that . . ." or "When Jimmy does that, you believe it's . . ." is a useful way to begin.

After the second person speaks, the first should repeat the latest viewpoint to make sure it too has been not only heard but understood.

2. Try to find the common ground between both viewpoints.

3. If areas of disagreement remain, try to define exactly what these are without belittling or ridiculing. If spouses differ on child-rearing techniques or philosophy, often the reason lies not in some mysterious or worthless stubbornness but in their own rearing, which they are either reproducing or renouncing, depending on the quality of their own early years.

4. After discussing motives for your disagreement, try again to reach some common opinion on at least some portion of the problem.

5. Next try to achieve a decision for action or, failing that, several feasible preliminary suggestions: which parent will implement which, and when.

6. If you run a busy household where work always needs doing, be kind to yourself and schedule your discussion with your spouse for a time when the TV set is off, the children are out or alseep, and you are not trying to prepare or eat dinner.

SUPERSEDING EMOTION

Occasionally a child's phobic symptom may not appear because he is exhibiting another symptom. Common examples of "phobic coverup" involve depression or anxiety reactions. Misreading the phobic child and therefore forcing him to perform in the dreaded situation can result in severe acting out.

THE DEPRESSED AND FEARFUL CHILD

Depression in a child looks different from adult depression. In both, nevertheless, the causes (motivation) usually involve a loss. When parents separate or divorce, depression can occur. If the child loses a friend or a dog, changes school or experiences the death of someone close, depression may result.

Depression is usually accompanied by a noticeable change in performance. Grades may worsen; teachers may report a change in attitude, including greater distractibility at school. Instead of the morose, energyless state of an adult, however, a child can exhibit the following symptoms:

· Sleep problems	Either difficulty in falling asleep or waking in the middle of the night
· Eating problems	Either overeating or loss of appetite
· Anhedonia	Loss of pleasure in previously enjoyed activities
· Hyperactivity	Increase in activity level accompanied by high distractibility and difficulty concentrating
· Increased aggression	Fighting with peers at school or home.

What to Do

1. Consider your child's surface state or behavior—any of the above symptoms of depression—as a statement he is trying to make about an underlying problem, which is the fear or phobia.

2. Learn all you can about your child's reaction to, or avoidance of, the particular phobic situation.

3. Do not force the child to enter the feared area.

4. If the problem persists, see your pediatrician.

THE LYING OR DENYING CHILD

Boys who worry about "looking chicken"—or have learned that "real men" are never afraid—aptly fit this description. If such a child fears snakes or a zoo visit, he will hide this emotion behind ridicule or sarcasm when invited to accompany his father: "The snake house? That's the dumbest thing I ever heard. Who cares about stupid snakes?"

Although we live in a culture that still considers fears in girls more acceptable than in boys, a ten-year-old girl may be ashamed to admit even to herself that she fears the dark, animals, or something else that "only babies" worry about.

What to Do

1. Keep your temper. This child will seem unreasonable as well as ungrateful when refusing invitations that involve the phobic situation.

2. If you sense that fear underlies the ridicule, say that everybody is afraid sometimes; some fears are useful because they keep us safe from harm; and nobody need be ashamed of feeling afraid.

3. Be sensitive to the child's needs without spoiling him or surrendering to every whim.

4. Encourage your child to speak about feelings and listen with an open mind.

5. Avoid stereotypes about what "real men" (or women) do, since they imply that anyone who doesn't conform is hopeless.

6. Don't force the phobic child into the dreaded situation.

7. Do seek proessional help for the lying or denying child, especially if the fear has reached phobic proportions.

SECONDARY GAIN

The child (or adult) who manages in various ways to turn an affliction to his long-term benefit is apt to be timid, shy, dependent, immature, introverted, even hypochondriacal. At some level the family system or culture of this child is supporting the development or maintenance of such a phobia. Examples involve the child who sees mother getting solid attention for fearing bugs, mice, dizziness, or heart palpitations and cannot resist trying out the same symptoms. Other familiar examples stem from the kind of religious beliefs that glorify suffering or from the kind of family that notices its members only when they do or have something wrong.

In more normal families, the child who, when tumbled by an ocean wave, is scooped up by a watchful parent who makes the experience a *game* is less likely to become phobic than the child whose parent reacts to a minor upset as if it were a four-alarm crisis. Whereas the former parent will say "Let's try the water again and learn how to take the waves," the latter will declare they must leave the water or even the beach. This phenomenon partly explains why two children, exposed to the same stimulus, do or do not acquire a phobia.

The secondary gain reaped by the phobic child involves, of course, augmented or redoubled parental attention, which the youngster then finds nearly impossible to relinquish.

What to Do

1. Reread the beginning of Chapter 8 on how to distinguish a fear from a phobia.

2. The pediatrician remains your best first stop for any emotional symptom that is interfering with normal life. Ask the doctor's advice, including a recommendation for further professional help if needed.

3. Effective, short-term ways to treat and conquer phobias now exist. See the Afterword on behavioral therapy techniques and Chapter 7 for information on drugs that improve or eliminate the anxiety underlying school phobia while the child continues the therapy sessions.

4. Examine how your own family or cultural dynamics may be contributing to a child's problem. The aim here is to admit what is happening and work with or around it—not to blame yourself, your partner, or your parents for the fact that it exists.

5. Aid your child's recovery by letting him do—with your help or supervision—any reasonable activity of which he once seemed hopelessly afraid. Stress how brave he now is—instead of how dangerous you may still regard the activity, especially if it involves something you may also fear. Your goal as a parent should be to produce an independent human being at some appropriate age for this, not one who clings to you from terror of the world or one who gets messages that "halfway better" is about as much or as far as anybody can expect in this uncertain world.

THE GIFTED AND AFRAID

Gifted children are a group unto themselves. With an I.Q. of 130 and above, they are bright, curious, active, and creative. On the other side, they may also be hyperactive, easily bored, stubborn, and ingenious beyond their years at devising excuses. Intellectually ahead of their peers, they are apt to lag behind them, however, in social skills, since they miss cues and evoke reactions that make other children avoid them. To the extent that schools and society cater to the "normal," to that extent can the genius or the extremely talented find themselves extremely unhappy and fearful over their social and psychological distance from other people and over what appears to be their "lopsided" skills.

What to Do

1. Know that proper testing (to determine in which areas your child excels) and proper schooling (to evoke and utilize that excellence) are the keys here.

2. Since gifted children share with phobics the tendency to a vivid "what-if" imagination, listen carefully to what your child says about the feared situation.

3. Seek professional help for any fear that is verging on phobia.

THE OBSESSIVE-COMPULSIVE AND AFRAID

Obsessive-compulsive behavior is one more system of isolating anxiety that resembles in form the phobic response. In order to function at all—to approach the social or physical situation about which he has overwhelming anxiety—this child projects such feelings onto an object, which can then be isolated and "tamed" through a series of rituals.

One example of an obsessive-compulsive boy is a youngster who at the age of eleven began touching whatever he passed. If he was passing a fence, he needed to touch every board or post, not just once but a specific number of times, or he would grow most anxious, fearing something terrible would result from such "lapse."

Next the behavior generalized to house inspections before he retired at night. Each closet and door had to be examined against visitors or intruders, again a specific number of times. The onset of these rituals occurred shortly after the boy failed acceptance at the private school that three of his friends would attend.

During several months of a therapy group he learned a different way to handle his terror and other feelings. His gesturing thus decreased significantly.

What to Do

1. Know that certain children with a phobia will camouflage it behind rituals that others find odd or annoying.

2. Know that ritualistic behavior, such as avoiding sidewalk cracks or walking only on certain streets, is normal, however, in eight- through ten-year-olds.

3. Seek professional help for the phobic child trapped in a habit or ritual that interferes with everyday life.

FOODS, ALLERGIES, AND BEHAVIOR

As you will see in the Afterword, many fear reactions—and all the phobias—profoundly affect the body as well as the mind through the sympathetic nervous system, which controls the "fight or flight" response.

For this to occur, one important pathway involves nutrition. There are many explanations for the causes of various behaviors. One theory, which is gaining popularity now and should be further investigated, is the effect of specific food consumption or allergy upon behavior. As every parent knows, a hungry child can be a cranky one, apt to overreact to any stimulus.

That foods eaten (or omitted) may affect brain function and behavior is an ancient idea now being reexamined in light of newest discoveries about the action of hormones and other substances upon biochemical pathways within different portions of the brain.

Proper nutrition involves sensible selection and rotation of foods to maximize energy and minimize possible development of allergies and other autoimmune problems (the body fighting itself). Here is the opinion of Dr. Ray Wunderlich, author of *Allergy, Brains, and Children Coping:*

> Allergy can interfere with the function of the brain, and the brain that doesn't work properly can bring on allergy. There is a growing realization that the adjustment problems of children are more often biologically based than we commonly recognized in the past. The ability of tranquilizers, anticonvulsants, stimulants, vitamins, and minerals to alter brain function leads us to look for further explanations of behavior within the child, at the cellular level.

To summarize this idea: If the forebrain is not properly nourished, the animal, emotional brain(s) can take over.

CHAPTER 12

. . .

Beyond the Bogeyman: Donna and the Arrow

People are disturbed not by things, but by the views they take of them.

—EPICTETUS, first century A.D.

Recently Donna, a writer and teacher, attended a Manhattan workshop on techniques of successful selling—not because she was eager for the topic or even curious about the leader but because one of her friends, who'd helped organize the day, said they needed attendees.

The leader, Robert Kiyosaki from San Diego, declared that the initial and, indeed, chief step toward successful selling—and one of the things they would learn that day—was how to overcome fear. Fear, he said, stands for False Evidence Appearing Real.

To demonstrate, Mr. Kiyosaki had his assistant hold a most lethal-looking, steel-tipped arrow parallel to the floor at neck height. After some meditation Mr. Kiyosaki walked straight into the arrow while everyone held his breath. Donna actually saw the steel tip hit the soft part of the man's neck, right above the collarbone. His blood, however, did not gush messily to end both the workshop and his life; indeed, the arrow did not even pierce his neck. Instead, its wooden shaft cracked with a loud snap. Holding the pieces in his hand, he then said, "I'm here to tell you that before the end of the day all of you will be able to do this too."

Everybody groaned. And Donna's immediate emotional response was typical, "No way will he get *me* to walk into that arrow. Never," she thought. Recalling what she knew of this man—his work in neurolinguistic programming (mind-body-speech control) and his study of the incredible art of firewalking with Tony Robbins—she also guessed that such talents can take months or years to perfect.

"We'll begin now," Mr. Kiyosaki announced, "but remember, you don't have to do it unless you really want to."

"Well," thought Donna grudgingly. "Since I'm here, I'll listen to what he's got to say."

"Close your eyes," he said. "Now remember a time when you felt totally successful at something you were trying to do. Perhaps the first big project you tried on your own as a child or maybe something more recent. Put in all the sensory details —how the experience, the room, the people sounded, felt, even smelled or tasted.

"Now make a fist; nod your head; and say 'yes' out loud."

Since this didn't seem very threatening—her recalled experience indeed had been a moment of triumph in her life—after some indecision Donna imagined her scene. It involved descending in an elevator from the office of an editor, who had just enthusiastically offered to buy the manuscript of Donna's first book. Donna again saw herself in the building lobby as she hurried to the phone bank to inform her husband, also a writer, of her Big News.

Having embellished her scene further, Donna made a fist, nodded, and murmured, "Yes."

Already Mr. Kiyosaki was continuing. "Next imagine a time when you felt totally loved, maybe during your childhood, maybe something more recent. Again make a fist; nod your head; and say yes."

This time a scene sprang so instantly to mind that she couldn't help wondering why she found it easier to remember being loved than being successful. When Donna was small and her parents lacked money to attend movie theaters, they did manage to make family outings to a drive-in theater, for which Donna and her sister prepared by donning pajamas before setting off. Her tranceful memory showed her father carrying her into the house and putting her to bed while her head drooped, half asleep, on his comforting shoulder.

Again Donna followed the directions about sensory details, fist making, and saying yes.

Mr. Kiyosaki then asked the group, "What is the thing in your life you're most afraid of? . . . Are you willing to let go of that fear?"

A few people answered, "Yes."

Having imagined her worst fear—that of success, of her own power to get and accomplish what she wanted—Donna suddenly decided she *was* very tired of it, would, in fact, be glad to let it go.

But how?

"Write your fear on a piece of paper. Now, anybody who wants to do this, take one arrow from this box, and wrap your paper around your arrow."

After everybody, including Donna, had done that, he reached the challenging part of the program. "All those who want to try, look up and visualize your successful and your loved times. Next you will begin walking into your arrow that my assistant will hold for you. While you do it, you will visualize pulling all your energy into yourself."

Again everyone groaned, but Donna thought, "Well, I've come this far. I can always reach the arrow and chicken out if I want."

Trying to obey all his directions, she strode forward into the arrow wrapped with the paper on which was written her special fear. Suddenly she heard a crack! Feeling her throat, she discovered no blood, not even a scratch. Yet she must have done it! She stared down at the broken halves of the arrow in her hand.

First she hadn't believed she could do it. Now she couldn't believe she had done it.

Mr. Kiyosaki continued the seminar. "If your worst fear ever again haunts you, say to yourself, 'If I've done this' (waving pieces of broken arrow), 'how can I be afraid of—whatever it is?' "

When the day's workshop ended, Donna took her arrow home and tried the sharp steel tip against a finger with no mental preparation. It hurt and, had she continued, could easily have drawn blood. To this day, she wonders how she actually walked into a lethal arrow without the slightest harm. Also to this day she keeps it in full view tacked onto the bulletin board in her office.

· · ·

By now, you probably wonder what this anecdote, true but improbable, has to do with your child's fear or phobia. Assuming that many fears and especially phobias are not innate—that we *learn* them through bad experiences, accidents, miscalculations—implies that what is learned can be *unlearned* with proper reeducation, someone who cares, someone (like Mr. Kiyosaki or another therapist) who knows enough of the human psyche to coax even the initially unwilling into the nearly impossible.

Because mind control forms part of this, we have equipped you as much as possible with phrases to use when talking with your child, phrases she can then use to combat the fear. Because body control (action) forms the rest of the war on fear, we have also stressed appropriate tasks you and your child can do to fight ghosts at four or school refusal at fourteen.

Chapter 1 of this book states some alarming statistics, particularly about the millions of probably housebound agoraphobics and others whose lives are crippled by "cannots" and "darenots" of fears they might have outgrown—if anyone had known or cared to help when the fear first started.

Some fears about, for example, heights, dark streets, or toothy animals are real and sensible. Others are just False Evidence Appearing Real. We thus hope this book will help you and your child distinguish and discuss—and then act effectively. The rewards are a more independent life for both of you and the certain knowledge that you have succeeded at some of parenthood's challenging tasks.

· · ·

Can you guess by now what (according to Jerome Kagan, Harvard University) are any of the five "ideal qualities" desired by most U.S. parents? In *The Nature of the Child* he also contrasts these with other cultures where prime childhood virtues are loyalty to family, religious piety, and development of specific talents, including physical prowess.

The "American virtues" for children are autonomy, intelligence, humanness, sociability, and—control of fear.

Afterword:
When Professional
Help Is Needed

By Dr. Robert Schachter

BEHAVIOR MODIFICATION

Because fear is so primitive, yet complex, an emotion, it has been studied extensively until it has attracted many theories of causation. Fear is a valuable emotion, helping us respond to danger by mobilizing our bodies physically and mentally. Furthermore, the fears of very young children, such as anxiety over separation or strangers, are adaptive; that is, they help the infant survive. And many fears evolve developmentally when the infant or child discovers new skills (crawling, running) to accomplish feats hitherto impossible. As the child learns to walk and finds he can physically leave mother, separation anxiety develops. His reaction is not unreasonable—if he does wander quietly away, he does, in fact, soon find himself lost and helpless.

Certain fears are inborn or genetically part of our mammalian heritage. In his book *Fears and Phobias,* Dr. Isaac Marks discusses the evolutionary and genetic characteristics of fear, including the famous observations by anthropologist Konrad Lorenz. When a monoplane model was moved above their heads, newly hatched ducks and geese showed fear because this terrifying model resembled a short-necked bird of prey in flight. Although the hatchlings had never seen a hawk or falcon before, they knew enough to fear its look-alike. When the lighting was changed, however, to cast a shadow resembling a long-necked bird like the parents they likewise never had seen, they showed no escape behavior.

Another series of fascinating experiments, performed by Eleanor Gibson and R. D. Walk, created the false "visual cliff" (a foot-high glass platform divided into halves, one cloth-covered, the other transparent; see Chapter 5, Spatial Fear: Heights). Several species, including chicks, monkeys, goats, and human infants aged six to fourteen months, avoided the "deep" (transparent) side but crawled on the solid-looking half.

Fear of snakes is indigenous to many species, regardless of whether they live anywhere near the tropical or rocky habitats of poisonous reptiles. Thus many humans, who will never see a snake outside a zoo, fear them anyway.

Other fears, based on actual trauma, develop in response to the pain or accident produced by a concrete situation or experience. In this book many anecdotes involving, as examples, the dentist, animals, or storms, show the birth of this sort of fear. Such fears matter because they are precisely the ones that can develop into phobias if not properly treated.

To summarize, fear is useful when it is physically arousing, adaptive (survival-related), innate, or related to normal development. Fear based on traumatic incidents can also be useful, provided it neither generalizes nor develops into phobia.

Phobias are the fears that disturb a person's daily functioning as he goes to any length to avoid the dreaded object or situation and, finally, the panicky emotions associated with it.

Although an older child may try to conceal such fear, it nevertheless affects the life of everyone in the family.

In the panic attacks accompanying phobia, the body over-
mobilizes to the point of near collapse—hyperventilation,
rapid, even irregular heart action, sweating, dizziness, blurred
vision, "jelly legs"—the spectrum of symptoms already listed
in this book.

The fear or phobia "habit" has, therefore, a physical basis.
It depends on pathways (circuits) established by learning and
repetition along and among nerve cells within the nervous
system.

The prevalent theory by which to explain the existence of
phobias involves this *conditioning*—that certain fears are a conditioned response produced by a stimulus (the feared object).
Another way to say this is that, in some situations, we *learn* to
be afraid. This theory can account for many fearful responses,
particularly those associated with large or small traumas—the
kind that produce phobias and require treatment in some children. Treatments for the phobic child have ranged from drug
therapy to long-term psychotherapy.

One of the most effective is behavior therapy, by which the
child "unlearns" the fear by acquiring new ways to cope with
it. Behavior therapy assumes that an event has been paired
with a fearful response. The goal of this approach is to relieve
the symptom by teaching an alternative response.

The phobic response is a pattern that develops most often
by accident but that gets reinforced until it occurs habitually.
An example is a seven-year-old boy who, after being upended
by a powerful undertow at the seashore, develops a fear of
waves that generalizes to a phobia of all large bodies of water.

To alleviate the phobic behavior, the behavioral therapist
attempts to help the phobic person learn a different pattern by
pairing a pleasant stimulus to the feared situation (see later on
in this chapter). This concept, introduced by Joseph Wolpe, is

called *operant conditioning.* And it is based on the nineteenth-century work, now called *classical conditioning,* of the Russian scientist Ivan Pavlov, who experimented with animals.

A rat, for instance, may be in a cage with an electrified floor through which mild shocks can be delivered. The cage may also contain a lever to turn off the shocks. If a tone is sounded just before the shock (painful stimulus) occurs, the animal will soon fear the tone as much as shock. This is one example of classical conditioning to produce fear.

Classical conditioning, as initiated by Pavlov, involved teaching a dog to salivate upon the hearing of a tone. By pairing a tone with a morsel of a food (pleasant stimulus), Pavlov accomplished a conditioned response in the dog until the animal would salivate at the tone alone—with no food. This artificial effect was both caused and manipulated by the experimenter.

From classical conditioning, it was learned that such responses could be reinforced to shape behavior. That is, the rat learned to terminate or avoid shock by pressing a lever in the cage; indeed, it soon did this upon merely hearing the tone that signaled the fear response—*before* the shock could occur. (Do you recall the adage "Once warned, twice shy"?) The termination or avoidance of shock thus became the reinforcer in the event, as food is in other animal experiments when the animal, tempted by food, learns to reenter without fear a formerly shocking situation.

HOW EFFECTIVE IS BEHAVIORAL THERAPY, COMPARED WITH OTHER METHODS?

Various sets of statistics exist, compiled by many schools and groups that advocate everything from biofeedback to psychoanalysis. Although all achieve some measure of success against fears, enough to encourage each therapist to continue, it is probably what they share—some form of confidential interaction between patient and therapist or group—that gives them similar rates, namely about 50 percent of patients recovered or improved by the end of treatment.

By contrast, behavioral therapy, especially in the form when therapist both accompanies the patient and models appropriate behavior in the feared situation, has a much higher success rate. It reaches 80–90 percent, and it is maintained months and years after treatment. The usual division is that 50–60 percent report being "helped completely" (phobia eliminated), and about 30 percent report "moderate help," while only 3–6 percent report "no help." Behavioral therapy succeeds because it understands and works with the nature of the phobic process and because it provides concrete tools against the crisis situation.

The rate of 80–90 percent, which resulted from Joseph Wolpe's original work, has been corroborated through the years. For example, a six-month to four-year follow-up of fifty adult phobia clinics with hundreds of participants, held at the White Plains Hospital Phobia Clinic (White Plains, New York), is reported by Dr. Frederic Neuman and Dr. Manuel Zane in Neuman's book *Fighting Fear* (1985).

· · ·

Many youngsters who seek help are suffering. One interesting case concerned a young patient of mine named Jason who, having been trapped by a hostile neighbor in the elevator of his own apartment building, developed such an intense fear of elevators that he could no longer ride to the thirtieth floor, where he lived.

Jason's family, who lived on the whole top floor of an exclusive Boston apartment house, was feuding with another family. To reach the top floor, Jason's family had to take a private elevator that, of course, passed the floor owned by the other family. At the height of the tension, the neighbor woman stopped the elevator at her floor, trapping poor Jason as the door opened. Not only did she harangue and insult the boy, it was a full five minutes before she finished screaming and finally released the elevator.

Jason was terrified. Although he described the incident to his parents, they could do nothing about it. Shortly thereafter, he refused to enter the elevator to reach his apartment. If forced into it, he began to tremble, blanch, and show extreme anxiety. Luckily, he could tiptoe into a back service elevator, not controlled by his neighbor, to conquer the thirty flights, but his terror of the front elevator would not abate.

The treatment proved fascinating, although at first Jason would not even discuss the incident. Upon being questioned about it, he withdrew and showed considerable agitation. After several sessions twice a week, Jason consented to describe to me what had occurred. He was clearly suffering extreme anxiety that had become a phobia related to the incident.

The treatment plan involved his gradual acceptance of the fearful feelings that were paralyzing him. Together the boy and I accomplished this through the process of *systematic desensitization* (discussed later in this chapter).

The first task was to develop a hierarchy of fears related to the terrifying woman. He listed every scary association he had to her—seeing her on the street, getting into a car, within the building—and rated each fear from 1 to 100, according to scariness. The most horrific scene, of course, was to have her again stop the elevator with him in it. The mildest was a scene of her getting onto a plane and leaving the country.

The second step was to teach Jason a system of complete relaxation. He was asked to tense each muscle in his body progressively and then to relax it. For example, he would tighten his feet, hold the tension for ten seconds, and release. He would then tighten the muscles of his calves, hold these for ten seconds, and release. After finishing with the muscles of his face, he was in a relaxed state.

At this point a nonthreatening scene was described for him,

followed by a scene with the lowest fear rating, then a scene next highest on the scale. He was instructed that when he became anxious, he should raise one hand. On the third scene, he did so. When asked to relax again, he repeated the relaxation exercise until he felt calm. Again a threatening scene was introduced.

This process continued throughout half the session. The rest of the time he discussed other aspects of his life. As he did this, moreover, he began to develop defensive strategy against such an incident recurring. He rehearsed remarks he could say to the woman if she again cornered him.

After six weeks Jason was functioning well and had reduced his fears. Although not afraid of elevators in general, he still could not bring himself to ride the one on which his trauma had occurred.

The final step of therapy happened at his home; its goal was an actual ride in the infamous elevator. Jason did the relaxation exercise in his apartment with my help. He then explored in fantasy the experience of riding the elevator. After he felt calm, we rode up and down together several times. Finally, Jason rode alone.

That proved the end of a successful treatment for a problem that not only afflicted his childhood but could have generalized or recurred whenever he had to take an elevator to meet a threatening interview or person. Psychological literature contains numerous anecdotes of patients who miss job interviews, business meetings, dates, and other occasions because they dread either the elevator ride or the encounter toward which it is whisking them.

Jason stayed cured of his phobia.

·   ·   ·

If you find that your child, like Jason, is in need of professional help, keep in mind that all professionals are not the same. Also remember that the number of degrees on the wall does not mean that this is the best doctor for you. As a patient, you are in a difficult position. We are all taught to respect the judgment of the doctor. As a patient, as in all else, you should be an informed consumer. Inform yourself, ask questions, and be sure that both you and your child feel comfortable with the therapist. If you feel doubtful, see someone else before making a commitment.

To assess the severity or persistence of a child's problem, the rule is: Seek help promptly when the fear

- begins to generalize from the situation where it originated or
- significantly hampers the child's and your family's daily life.

YOUR CHILD, THE THERAPIST, A PHOBIA CENTER

At the Children's Phobia Center in New York, the following procedure is used with good results. When a child is referred by a pediatrician or other professional, the parents are encouraged to come without the child for one or two meetings (about an hour each). During these periods the therapist takes a full history to learn the child's behavior from birth to the present. The phobic behavior, of course, is described and examined in detail—when it began, how often it was exhibited, how severe, where it occurred, and so on—whatever sheds light on the particular child's pattern of avoidance of some situation or object.

The child then has an interview to assess such symptoms within the context of the entire family system. To complete a diagnosis may require more than one meeting.

After determining a diagnosis, the therapist establishes a treatment plan. This states both short- and long-term treatment goals and defines how they may be accomplished. The therapist next discusses both the diagnosis and the treatment plan with the parents.

Depending on the nature of the child's problem, various approaches are usually offered. Sometimes treatment consists of seeing the parents alone or the entire family for several meetings to discuss strategies by which to minimize the phobic behavior. With school phobia, for instance, such strategies usually succeed.

Sometimes the therapist sees the child alone for a period of time, followed by meetings with the parents. During the child's visits, he is taught a method of systematic desensitization, which has become the primary procedure used to treat most phobias today. With it, the therapist teaches the child a different response to the feared situation. This occurs by gradually exposing the child's imagination to phobic stimuli along a hierarchy ("What frightens you least? Most? What experience is in between?") while simultaneously giving the child a contrasting experience, such as a method to relax. Using information from both child and parents, a hierarchy of fear is thus developed—a list or series of dreaded objects ranging from least to most feared.

The youngster is then taught how to relax by progressively flexing, tensing, and releasing muscles from the feet to the face. While relaxed, he is asked to imagine the least-feared situation. When this arouses anxiety, the therapist returns the child to the relaxed state. Then he imagines the next most frightening incident and is helped to relax until the scale is climbed, and the child can tolerate the most frightening thought. The parent later helps the child apply this method in the actual situation, or the child may apply it himself. Regular, deep breathing and positive imaging also aid the therapy.

Researcher and psychologist Joseph Wolpe developed the technique, terming it *reciprocal inhibition,* by which a pleasant stimulus (relaxation) is paired with a frightening one. It obtains symptomatic relief from most feared situations.

At the Center we have found that Kinetic Psychotherapy (KPT) is the follow-up tool that effectively helps the child remain phobia-free after phobic symptoms subside.

KPT is a specific group therapy approach I have developed (see Schachter 1974, 1978, and 1984); although not central to treating phobias, it is unique and has become a valuable tool to prevent relapse. This form of therapy was originally developed to help children who had difficulty identifying or verbalizing feelings. Knowing that all children who have experienced phobic episodes have much in common, we place them in such a group for a short period of time where they can discuss and continue using alternative modes of coping. The therapist guides and facilitates each of these groups.

The method uses a series of children's games similar to those played on the playground. Each game is modified to mimic, in feeling and tone, real-life situations. As a child plays, three events occur. First, the child experiences feelings. Next, he assumes a characteristic manner of coping, acting, and reacting, just as in real life. The child then associates to other times when he has felt similarly.

An example is the child's game of Keepaway. In this exercise, five youngsters pass around a ball and attempt to keep it away from another who stands in the middle of the circle. As the youngster in the middle begins to feel, he acts in a characteristic way. A youngster who strikes out when frustrated may strike out upon experiencing the frustration of five-against-one.

If this occurs, the game is stopped. The other children in the group are then used to show him an alternative way to handle the situation *at the instant* when the feeling occurs that triggers the behavior. Thus, the child quickly learns contrasting behaviors to add to a repertoire of coping skills. He also can share with others who have played the game and have had similar experiences.

The child is then asked to think of other times when he has

felt similarly. He immediately associates to other situations and can speak about this in the group. Using this approach, we have noted that 80 percent of the youngsters in treatment change their behavior within six to twelve months.

·

Fear
Survey
Chart

·   ·

·

	6 MO.	8 MO.	YR. 1	YR. 2	YR. 3	YR. 4	YR. 5
Separation Anxiety		X	X	X			
Stranger Anxiety	X						
Fear of Noises		X				X	X
Fear of Falling	X	X					
Fear of Animals		X			X	X	X
Fear Due to Inconsistent Discipline				X			
Fear Due to Toilet Training				X	X		
Fear of Bath		X	X				
Fear of Bedtime				X	X	X	
Fear of Doctor		X	X				
Fear of Monsters and Ghosts					X	X	X
Fear of Bed-wetting					X	X	
Fear of Crippled People					X	X	
Fear of Getting Lost							X
Fear of Going to Day Care				X			X
Fear of Loss of Parent						X	X
Fear of Death						X	X
Fear of Injury							X
Fear of Being Late to School							
Fear of Social Rejection							
Fear of Criticism							
Fear of New Situations							
Fear of Adoption							
Fear of Burglars							
Fear of Kidnapping							
Fear of Being Alone in the Dark							
Fear of Injections							
Fear of Heights							
Fear of Terrorism							
Fear of Plane or Car Crashes							
Fear of Sexual Relations							
Fear of Drug Use							
Fear of Public Speaking							
Fear of School Performance							
Fear of Crowds							
Fear of Gossip							
Fear of Divorce						X	X
Fear of Personal Danger							
Fear of War							

YR. 6	YR. 7	YR. 8	YR. 9	YR. 10	YR. 11	YR. 12	YR. 13	YR. 14	YR. 15	YR. 16
	X									
X	X				X	X				
		X								
X	X									
X										
	X									
X										
X		X						X	X	X
	X									
		X								
		X								
		X								
		X								
		X							X	
						X		X	X	
					X	X			X	X
					X			X	X	
							X	X	X	X
								X	X	X
									X	X
								X	X	
								X	X	
								X	X	X
								X	X	X
								X	X	X
								X	X	X
X	X	X	X	X	X	X	X	X	X	X
	X	X	X	X	X	X	X	X		
		X	X	X	X	X	X	X		

Bibliography

BOOKS

Bedford, Stewart. *Instant Replay*. New York: Institute for Rational Living, 45 East 65th Street, 10021, 1974. (Part of excellent parent-and-child guide series, *Rational-Emotive Educational Materials*.)

Berne, P., and L. Savary. *Building Self-Esteem in Children*. New York: Continuum Publishing Corp., 1981.

Brazelton, T. Berry. *To Listen to a Child: Understanding the Normal Problems of Growing Up*. New York: Addison-Wesley, 1984.

DuPont, Robert. *Phobia: A Comprehensive Summary of Modern Treatments*. New York: Brunner Mazel, 1982.

Gesell, Arnold. *The First Five Years of Life*. New York: Harper, 1940.

————, and Frances Ilg. *The Child from Five to Ten*. New York: Harper & Row, 1946.

————, Francis Ilg, and Louise Bates Ames. *The Years from Ten to Sixteen*. New York: Harper, 1956.

Gittelman-Klein, Rachel, ed. "Childhood Anxiety Disorders: Correlates and Outcome" in *Anxiety Disorders of Childhood*. New York: Guilford Press, 1985, pp. 101–25.

————. "Separation Anxiety in School Refusal and Its Treatment with Drugs" in L. Hersov and I. Berg, eds., *Out of School*. London: John Wiley & Sons, 1980, pp. 321–41.

Hechinger, Grace. *How to Raise a Street-Smart Child*. New York: Ballantine/Fawcett Crest, 1984.

Kagan, Jerome. *The Nature of the Child*. New York: Basic Books, 1984.

Kellett, Michael. *The Practical Storybook*, vols. 1 and 2. Hoptacong, NJ: Creative Learning Services, 102 Grenoble Place, 07843, 1982 and 1983. (Useful parent-and-child series for help with various common situations and emotions, including fears.)

Levinson, Harold. *Phobia-Free.* New York: Evans and Co., 1986.

Lewis, M., and Rosenblum, L., eds. *The Origins of Fear.* Origins of Behavior series, vol. 2. New York: John Wiley & Sons, 1974.

Marks, Isaac, *Fears and Phobias.* New York: Academic Press, Inc., 1969.

———. *Living with Fear.* New York: McGraw-Hill, 1978.

McCandless, Boyd R., and Trotter, Robert J. *Children, Behavior and Development,* 3rd ed. New York: Holt, Rinehart, and Winston, 1977.

Neuman, Frederic. *Fighting Fear: An 8-Week Guide to Treating Your Own Phobias.* New York: Macmillan, 1985.

Ready-Set-Grow Library, various titles including *Handling Your Up and Downs.* Columbus, OH: Weekly Reader Books, 4343 Equity Drive, P.O. Box 16717, 43216, 1986.

Schaefer, Charles. *How to Help Children with Common Problems.* New York: New American Library, 1982.

Tuan, Yi-fu. *Landscapes of Fear.* New York: Pantheon, 1979.

Waters, Virginia. *Color Us Rational.* New York: Institute for Rational Living, 1979. (Delightful coloring and story book to help children cope with emotions, including fear.)

———. *Fear Interferes.* New York: Institute for Rational Living, 1980. (Part of parent-and-child pamphlet series on teaching emotional skills involving fear, anger, self-acceptance, frustration tolerance, problem solving, and rational thinking.)

Wolman, Benjamin. *Children's Fears.* New York: Grosset & Dunlap, 1978.

Wolpe, Joseph. *Our Useless Fears.* Boston: Houghton Mifflin, 1981.

Wood, John. *What Are You Afraid Of?* Englewood Cliffs, NJ: Prentice-Hall, 1976.

Wunderlich, Ray. *Allergy, Brains, and Children Coping.* St. Petersburg, FL: Johnny Reads Press, 1973.

Zane, Manuel, and Milt, Harry. *Your Phobia: Understanding Your Fears Through Contextual Therapy.* New York: American Psychiatric Association, 1984.

ARTICLES AND JOURNALS
(ONLY INITIAL AUTHORS LISTED)

Bamber. J. H. "The Fears of Adolescence." *Journal of Genetic Psychology* 125:127–40, 1974.

Bauer, D. H. "An Exploratory Study of Developmental Changes in Children's Fears." *Journal of Child Psychology and Psychiatry* 17:69–74, 1976.

Bridges, Katherine M. B. "Emotional Development in Early Infancy." *Child Development* 3:324–41, 1932.

Cherry, Laurence. "The Good News about Depression." *New York* 19:22, 32–42, 6/2/1986.

Croake, J. W. "Fears of Children." *Human Development* 12:239–47, 1969.

Eme, R. "The Stability of Children's Fears." *Child Development* 49(4):1277–9, 1978.

Gordon, Edmund, ed. *American Journal of Orthopsychiatry.* New York: American Orthopsychiatric Association, 1775 Broadway, 10019. (Sensible, readable articles from multidisciplinary perspectives in mental health and human development; theme issues and much on therapeutic work with children and adolescents.)

Graziano, A. M. "Behavioral Treatment of Children's Fears: A Review." *Psychological Bulletin* 86:4, 804–30, 1979.

Jersild, A. T. "Methods of Overcoming Children's Fears." *Journal of Psychology* 1:75–104(b), 1935.

Maurer, A. "What Children Fear." *Journal of Genetic Psychology* 106:265–77, 1965.

Miller, Lovick C. "Factor Structure of Childhood Fears." *Journal of Consulting and Clinical Psychology* 39:264–68, 1972.

Miller, Sally R. "Children's Fears: A Review of the Literature with Implications for Nursing Research and Practice." *Nursing Research* 28:4, 7–8/1979.

Ollendick, T. H. "Fears in Children and Adolescents: Normative Data." *Behavioral Research Therapy* 23(4): 405–7, 1985.

Rachman, S. "The Aetiology and Treatment of Children's Phobias: A Review." *American Journal of Psychiatry* 118:95–105, 1961.

Schachter, R. S. "Kinetic Psychotherapy in the Treatment of Children." *American Journal of Psychotherapy* 28:430–37, 1974.

———. "Kinetic Psychotherapy in the Treatment of Families." *Family Coordinator* 283–88, 1978.

———. "Kinetic Psychotherapy in the Treatment of Depression in Latency Age Children." *International Journal of Group Psychotherapy* 34(1):83–91, 1984.

Staley, Arlinda A. "A Developmental Analysis of Mothers' Reports of Normal Children's Fears." *Journal of Genetic Psychology* 144:165–78, 1984.

Torgersen, S. "The Nature and Origin of Common Phobic Fears." *British Journal of Psychiatry* 134:343–51, 1979.

Wolpe, Joseph, and Lang, P. J. "A Fear Survey Schedule for Use in Behavior Therapy." *Behavior Research and Therapy* 2:27–30, 1964.

Index

About the Authors

DR. ROBERT SCHACHTER is a licensed psychologist with training in individual, group, and family therapy in New York, California, and Massachusetts. He previously served as executive director of Barndom Associates for Personal Growth and Robert Schachter Associates, outpatient clinics for children and adolescents, and as a consultant to the Human Resource Institute of Boston. Dr. Schachter developed the concept of Kinetic Psychotherapy (KPT), a type of group therapy used in the treatment of phobias, about which he has published extensively and lectured nationally.

Currently, Dr. Schachter directs the Phobia Center for Children and Robert Schachter Associates in New York. He is the consultant psychologist to the Yoder School, for children with learning disabilities, and is on the faculty of Columbia College of Physicians and Surgeons, Columbia Presbyterian Hospital, Department of Psychiatry, where he teaches psychiatrists in training. He lives with his family in New York City.

CAROLE SPEARIN MCCAULEY has written many medical and computer nonfiction books as well as fiction and magazine articles. Five of her short pieces have won prizes in international contests, including Writers of the Future. Ms. McCauley edits manuals, briefs, and other manuscripts for IBM's Technical Publications, and does public relations writing and speaking for the A. P. John Institute for Cancer Research. She belongs to several writers' groups, including the National Writers Union.

Ms. McCauley now divides her time between Warwickshire, England, and Greenwich, Connecticut. She is mother to a seven-year-old son who yearns for a world without large dogs, dark rooms, and ghosts.